Rasul GOULIEV

PATH
to
DEMOCRACY

FATEFUL LESSONS
OF THE 20th CENTURY

LIBERTY PUBLISHING HOUSE
New York • 1997

Rasul Gouliev
Path to Democracy

Publisher Ilya. Levkov

Liberty Publishing House, Inc.
475 Fifth Ave., Suite 511
New York, NY 10017-6220
Tel.: (212) 213-2126
Internet address: http://www.liberty.way.com/
E-Mail: liberty@way.com

Cover design by Asya R. Kunik

Printed in the United States of America

ISBN 0-914481-86-X

CONTENTS

My main hope, my main goal, is freedom and happiness for the people of Azerbaijan. No power could force me off the path toward this goal.

Rasul Gouliev

PREFACE TO AMERICAN EDITION

For the reader of this book, a state based on democratic traditions and principles is a natural environment. This reader takes for granted an opportunity to express himself freely and realize his wishes, and rarely reflects on such a great benefit and achievement of human civilization as an opportunity to live and work in a democratic open society.

For seventy-four years, the Soviet Empire posed a real threat to the free world, forcing democracies to spend their material and moral resources on defending civilization from a merciless, menacing power. Inherently destructive, antihuman in objectives that its apologists forced upon the world, this power emerged and triumphed in defiance of common sense, and embodied man's basest instincts. This power comprised every human sin in a concentrated form: envy of your neighbor's achievements; meanness toward beauty and luxury; servility to dictators; sloth and passivity in resolving the most complex problems of existence; ruthlessness toward independent thought; narrowness of mind; and deception without limit.

This social doctrine could attract only the most naive or ones with a distorted imagination.

Naturally, the democracies reacted with fear and took defensive measures to keep the virus infection of Communism out. Many a time was the civilized world shocked when the Communist leaders proclaimed their global goal: establishing a worldwide dictatorship of the proletariat. These proclamations were supported by the Soviet bayonets, as they cut a wide swath through the Middle and Far East, through Latin America and Africa, through Europe and Asia. Yet, following the laws of nature, sooner or later the bubble had to burst. And helped by fortunate circumstances, burst it did. The collapse of the Empire at the dawn of the 21st century heralded a new era: one of global openness of human civilization.

It might seem that, with victory achieved, the world can take a deep breath and focus on common problems: the environment, genetic and acquired diseases, and various humanitarian projects. Unfortunately, as has often happened in history, certain features of the old regime have persisted in newly independent states. Due to lack of a democratic tradition, these states were taken over by members of the former Communist elite, dictators vastly experienced in political intrigue. Disguised as democrats, they have successfully overcome the initial mistrust of the West and took their seats at the table of civilized nations. They clamored for social justice yesterday, and today they "affirm" free-world principles, while they continue to keep their people in spiritual and material slavery.

The post-Soviet dictators have preserved their Bolshevik essence, and their democratic facade can fool only the most gullible and forgetful person. Yet, regretfully, such gullibility and forgetfulness are characteristic not only of common folks, removed from political intrigue, but – in no lesser degree – of certain politicians. One gets the impression that today, as the global conflict between the Communist tyranny and civilized democracy has lost its urgency, these politicians have melted in the euphoria of the global collapse of totalitarianism and have lost their vigilance.

Even Zbigniew Brzezinski, as he tries to rationalize the reasons for the victories of the Communist ideology through such a long period, concludes that Communism

> ...had some similarities to the appeal of the great religions, each of which provided an over-arching explanation of what life is all about. ... But communism was not only a passionate response to deeply felt concerns or just a self-righteous creed of social hate. It was also a readily understandable system of thought, seemingly providing a unique insight into the future as well as the past.

Like many others who spent most of their adult lives in a totalitarian Communist state, I find this interpretation largely simplistic. More than anyone else, we would know that, rather than being a system of thought, Communism is a mechanism for suppressing the most elementary thinking. Communism is nothing but a set of dogmas and falsehoods, drilled into a person so hard as to preclude him from understanding their complete inanity. The slogans thus drilled were based on "combining" uncombinable notions, so as to befog the mind with complete illogicality and absurdity and thus pre-

9

vent any questions and doubts. You cannot pose a sane question to an insane statement.

Communist ideology makes a totalitarian regime far more dangerous, for such a state not only comprises the full set of measures aimed at suppressing free thought and intellect, but also a false ideology that is deeply inculcated in the minds of its bearers and executors. This is the reason why the dictators of the newly independent states, having taken down the old sign, continue to rule along basically unchanged ideological principles.

I agree with Winston Churchill, who long before the Soviet Empire came to its shameful end, had said tersely and precisely:"The day will come when it will be recognized without doubt through the civilized world that the strangling of Bolshevism at birth would have been an untold blessing to the human race."

This is why I wish that the Western reader not be misled by the facades and verbal demagogy employed by yesterday's Communist leaders. Personally responsible for the poisoning of minds and bodies of millions of their countrymen, they are still occupying the thrones on their respective shards of the Evil Empire; they are still working, by all imaginable and unimaginable means, to prolong the existence of the regimes restored on the national scale.

They are plunging their nations into a tragedy, and this tragedy is not so innocent and local. As recent history shows, such tragedies can spread into international ones. Hence we need to exercise extraordinary vigilance to prevent these tragedies from happening. Since our planet is one living organism, it is highly naive and simplistic to believe that a local hotbed of malignant disease cannot affect the world at large.

I want my reader to realize that the path chosen by the independent states formed on the ruins of the empire will affect not only their respective societies, but the entire world civilization – and that, reader, includes the fate of your children and grandchildren.

I want my reader to realize that by encouraging and stimulating new dictatorships, by prolonging their existence, we slow down the progress of civilization as we waste material and human resources – which affects your spiritual well-being as well.

I cannot imagine my contemporary, wherever he lives, remaining indifferent to the fate of fellow humans. There are no inherently backward or intellectually feeble nations: the problem lies with the regimes that drive their own people into misery. It is everybody's duty to help these people climb out of their hardship and render them moral and material support in building a historically justified democratic society.

I believe it is absurd to claim that setting up a dictatorship in a given country is a country's domestic affair. A country's domestic affair is to choose methods of implementing – not suppressing – democratic principles. Therefore, I believe, it is everybody's duty to speak up against the regimes that limit human rights and reject freedom of conscience and expression. Especially it is the duty of democratic institutions and the countries who have adopted international standards in upholding these principles.

There are many historical examples when the international community directly contributed to creating a democracy in a country. A vivid example is the Marshall Plan, which encouraged the establishment of democratic regimes in Western Europe and Japan. This example is especially apt and effective because economic assistance was directly linked to political transformations. However, one must act with extreme caution and consistence, since unfair discriminatory measures may negatively affect a democratic process. Such an example is US Congressional Amendment 907, which prohibits financing Azerbaijan on the national level, charging it with aggression – when 20 percent of Azerbaijan territory is occupied by Armenia, and a million Azerbaijani refuges have for years been without shelter and means of subsistence.

I want you to feel, upon reading this book, that there is a country called Azerbaijan, whose people can and want to be reliable partners. The descendants of those who, tens of thousands years ago, left unique carvings in Gobustan Caves; the descendants of Nizami and Fizuli; the children and grandchildren of the intelligentsia who fought the Russian Empire at the turn of the century; and, finally, those who, fighting the Soviet Empire, made sacrifices in the bloody events of January 1990 – they have earned their right to live in a free democratic society and build a common civilization alongside other free nations.

I call upon you not to remain, once again, indifferent to the fate of the nations who are deprived of their rights and are suffering under totalitarian regimes.

Finally, reader, I wish ardently that, having touched the fate of my people, you will raise your voice in defense of their rights and decency, of their historical future irrevocably linked to democracy and human progress. For, as Churchill said wisely:

> *Laws, just or unjust, may govern men's actions. Tyrannies may restrain or regulate their words. The machinery for propaganda may pack their minds with falsehood... But the soul of man thus held in trance or frozen in a long night can be awakened by a spark coming from God know where.*

TO THE READER

Through my entire life the freedom and happiness of the people of Azerbaijan have been my main hope and my objective. Short of death, no power can force me off this path.

Before embarking on an enterprise, any reasonable person should reflect on its results. I have wanted to write this book for a long time. During my years as the Chairman of the Azerbaijani Parliament, I repeatedly addressed such subjects as the nature of a democratic society, its advantages, and the impossibility of building a healthy law-abiding state based on semidemocracy/semidictatorship. My speeches were based on more than my personal experience; I had to pore over tens of thousands of pages on these subjects.

I categorically oppose the notion that the Azerbaijani people are incapable of accepting democracy and need to be taught it in a piecemeal manner.

First, up to now, the Azerbaijani people have never been presented with democracy and freedom, and therefore one cannot conclude whether they can accept it or not.

Besides, the notion that democracy should be introduced piecemeal is without foundation.

Both assumptions are absurd: who is to decide how long the democratization process should be stretched out? Five years? Ten – fifty – a hundred – a thousand? Who is to decide on the doses of democracy and their contents?

Democracy can exist only as a whole: either it exists, or it does not. The people who have suffered under a cruel totalitarian regime, deformed both in morality and in practice, will accept democracy in a natural fashion.

Finally, I categorically disagree with the opinion that the Azerbaijani people in their current stage are so inferior to 17th-century English or 18th-century Americans as to be unable to perceive concepts of democracy.

I disagree with the idea that building a democracy in our country would take centuries.

To the champions of this notion I can only say: Gentlemen! Truly democratic European society emerged only after World War II. After the war, West Germany was seized by famine and poverty, the country had limited natural resources, and yet in ten years their living conditions were twenty times higher than in today's Azerbaijan. Similar development took place in other European countries.

The sine qua non in building a truly democratic society consists in transformations in two parallel directions: democratization of politics and liberalization of the economy. Whoever persists in labeling these ideas radical either does not understand – or understands only too well – that the sole alternative is the totalitarian society.

15

From the very first days of our independence I came to realize that the idea of an open society would not be easy to implement. I did hope that once Ayaz Mutalibov – a man who does not belong in politics – was gone, democratic construction would get under way. Unfortunately, that was not to be.

To the contrary, the National Front leaders assumed that the main reason for Mutalibov's failure was excessive weakness of his leadership, and therefore tightened the screws and centralized the government. Yet in the absence of a clear-cut leader, this centralization was taken over by autonomous groups, which eventually led to their defeat.

In 1993–94, I was still hoping that, once the war was brought to an end, once the illegal military groups were disarmed, once the conditions favorable to illegal rackets were removed, a legitimate democratic state could emerge. I held on to this illusion up to April 1995, when the last illegal military group was disarmed. I assumed that the disarmament would be accompanied by democratic processes, which would encourage people to gradually improve their living conditions and give them a measure of confidence. At every session I tried to convince my fellow parliamentarians of the need for democratic development in politics and the economy.

Unfortunately, this did not happen. Beginning in May 1995, my hopes for democracy in Azerbaijan began waning, and by early 1996 they vanished altogether. While supporting the measures aimed at the strengthening of the state, I was equally vigorous in criticizing inaction in political and economic reform. I emphasize that from the very start I was profoundly in favor of taking the most radical action in disarming the bands and the rackets that were plotting coups d'état. I spent a considerable amount of personal effort in suppressing the attempts to overthrow the existing government by force. And I am still convinced that the measures taken in 1995–96 were absolutely necessary. But as time went along I came to realize that we were failing to achieve our objective: a genuinely free democratic society. The actual events took a different path and led to a stronger totalitarian regime. It turned out that the paths to two opposite objectives – democracy and totalitarianism – led through similar circumstances.

Now we can see the consequences that befell the Azerbaijani people: over 90 percent of the population live in poverty. Left without means of subsistence, unneeded in their land, Azerbaijanis emigrated. The population fell from 7.5 million to 5.5 million, as 2 million Azerbaijanis wandered off to Russia, Turkey, Iran, Ukraine, Central Asia, the Baltics, and Europe.

Unfortunately, their situation in these countries remains painful. For example, in Turkey, regardless of their occupation, Azerbaijanis' have wages that are one-half or even one-third of those paid the natives. Our teachers, doctors, and researchers are forced to take menial jobs. We know well of the repressions Azerbai-janis are subject to in Russia and other ex-Soviet countries. Yet not one of them returns: at home they are insulted and humiliated even worse, while in a foreign land they at least have a chance to earn a little money.

Long ago, at the turn of the century, workers from all over the world migrated to Baku for jobs; now

Azerbaijanis cannot find a place for themselves in their own country. Should a person choose to stay, he faces unemployment (which has doubled) or, should he find a job, the problem of making ends meet. How much of his miserly wage will he be actually paid and how will he support his family? How long should he suffer and starve and survive on the promises of the gushing oil and the wealth for the coming generations?

Some of those well entrenched in positions of power will surely say: Rasul Gouliev still insults the Azerbaijani people by calling them "miserable"; hence, the people must oppose him.

I can only say this: I, Rasul Gouliev, belong among the most miserable of my people.

Why?

How can I be happy if 20 percent of our land is still occupied by Armenian troops and if over a million refugees live below the most elementary human conditions?

How can I be happy if liberating these lands and returning of the refugees have come to a dead end, and can never be resolved under the current policy?

How can I be happy if my people receive the handouts of humanitarian aid (of which 70 percent is stolen by certain parties) and are turned into a nation of beggars? While my people develop a mentality of thinking it is better to beg than to earn?

How can I be happy if over 90 percent of our people live in misery?

How can I be happy if most Azerbaijani intellectuals have to sell their last belongings in order to feed their families?

18

How can I be happy if over two million of my people have been forced to seek employment abroad, despite humiliation and insults – because it is still better than what they get at home?

How can I be happy if my people, who have shed more blood than anyone else en route to freedom and democracy, who have been told that oil wealth is enough to cover the entire land with a 1-mm layer of gold – yet these people now find themselves in such deprivation?

How can I be happy if in the past five years about 100,000 children were born in tents or without a roof over their heads?

No, I cannot be happy if my people are doomed to suffering. Perhaps someone else can; but personal happiness of a few does not mean that the people as a whole are happy.

There is only one aspect in which the Azerbaijani people can feel "fortunate": no other people have been blessed with so many "supergenius" leaders. That's the way it has been through history: the Azerbaijani people have always lived much worse than others, but their leader has always been the most "brilliant" person in the world. Such is human destiny. One nation is blessed to be born, grow up, learn, work, and enjoy freedom along with all it brings; while a nation like mine remains deprived of earthly joys and has to comfort itself with the knowledge that it is being ruled by the most "brilliant" leader. Can this be the essence of our miserable life? Perhaps it is worth our while to trade our customary way of life for that of other nations unburdened by the "genius" of their leaders?

While conceiving this book, I realized that I was facing a campaign of hatred.

I foresee the following:

■ Persecution of my family and friends and even casual acquaintances.

■ A powerful campaign of slander against me personally: *Rasul has impoverished Azerbaijan by selling off the oil.* Many have already been jailed in order to "gather evidence" against me; now will be the time to spread it.

■ A tragicomic farce will be broadcast on TV: *We should have known the true nature of Rasul Gouliev, this Public Enemy No.1, who was quietly running his little con games. You have no idea what kind of crimes have been committed by his family and friends – now the truth can be told.*

■ They will insinuate I have bought half Baku's real estate, etc., etc.

Television will be a crucial medium in this campaign. The leitmotif will be: *Now that we have unearthed the worst traitor and his crimes, things will get better; just wait for another five years or so, and everything will get to normal.*

An integral part of this campaign will consist of age-old arguments aimed at shutting someone up: *Rasul Gouliev is in cahoots with our worst enemies – he is singing their song.* Then they will scream, *We're being criticized!*, making it sound like state treason; the meaning of the word we will be expanded from "the rulers" to "the people".

20

This is their logic: *Azerbaijan consists of "us" and our flunkeys; whatever is aimed at us is aimed at Azerbaijan.* This reasoning carefully omits the main objective of the book: to promote, in both its contents and its message, the happy future of the Azerbaijani people.

Ironically, before these officials came to power, they had accused their contemporary regime of far worse crimes than any enemy did. So, aren't they insulting the intelligence of our people by using such primitive tricks? Do they actually believe that Azerbaijanis cannot tell black from white; that all of them resemble such wretches as Fatma and Tukazban – characters created by our famous satirist Sabir in order to prick human vanity and help people get rid of the slave inside them?

However, I trust the wisdom and long-range vision of my people. The people can see and realize that Gouliev has been gone from the scene for over a year, yet the situation is not improving; to the contrary, it is deteriorating. The people will know that since 1992, i.e., the collapse of the Soviet Union and the formation of the independent Republic of Azerbaijan, Gouliev has not been engaged in any business activity. The people will see through the lies of these accusations, and I do not intend to furnish any extra evidence to the effect.

However, if we follow the statistics, we might posit that every nation contains at least one-tenth percent of base, vain people who sold their souls to the devil and have no moral values. We can find such individuals all across the social strata: intelligentsia, bureaucracy, workers, farmers. Elementary math will show that, if the Azerbaijani population is indeed 7.5 million, the number of these people will come up to 7,500. If about six of them a day speak on TV, then 2,190 of them will speak in a year, and it will take three and a half years of TV shows for all of them to denounce me. At the same time, following the system developed under Stalin, the authorities will organize rallies in the workplaces, in order to give this persecution an appearance of a popular campaign.

I doubt there are many people in Azerbaijan who will question my professional qualities. Thus I will have few problems providing myself, my family, and even my distant relatives with all they need. At the same time I will continue my charitable activity in the area of national health and education; I have helped our students abroad and will continue to do so, for it is my firm belief that our future as a nation is directly linked to our level of education. And I never turned down anyone for help. Thus, I will be easily able to have both a peaceful life and a good name.

Yet the current misery of the Azerbaijani people and the horrors that are about to befall them deprive me of this peace. If I remain silent, my conscience will be tainted forever, and I will be forever guilty in the face of my people. As a citizen aware of his duty, I am not afraid of the dangers to my life and my future; they are nothing compared with the dangers that are in store for my people.

If I should stand accused of pursuing a personal goal or a high position, I will say that careerism is not a part of my nature. I occupied one of the highest positions allowed for by the national Constitution; without resorting to the hypocrisy and conformism typical of some others, I could have simply toned down my protest, and still retained my position.

The attitude of our top officials toward power borders on the ridiculous. For example, if at a meeting someone says that a mutual friend has dreams of becoming President, the rest get agitated and begin calling him a traitor and an enemy of the people. According to this odd logic, it is shameful to want to be President. If so, the position of President is a shameful one, too. In normal countries, a person trying to become nominated for President enjoys popular respect. In Azerbaijan, such ambition is broadcast to people with disapproval.

Why am I telling you this? Because such disapproval has already been voiced at certain meetings. And I am sure that soon it will be made into nationwide disapproval.

Therefore I would like to assure my readers that the happiness of the Azerbaijani people is my only goal, and I will do everything in my power to reach it, whether someone likes it or not.

As for the slander of my good name, I will try to do all I can to draw the attention of the international community and law-monitoring organizations to the lies about me being circulated and the pressure being exercised on my family, relatives, friends, and supporters.

It is fine that we call ourselves a democratic country and have signed the documents adopted by the international community. But the main thing is to observe them.

As I address my fellow citizens, I exhort them not to fall for these devilish provocations and decide for themselves what is true and what is not. I could analyze the events taking place in Azerbaijan and I could cite specific examples to show how the Azerbaijani people have been driven to the limit and who has caused their impoverishment. Yet, since it may hurt the public image of our country, I will not do so for the moment.

The purpose of this book is not to expose specific persons. I can only hope that it will make the reader think and understand that the future of the people is linked to democracy, and nothing else but democracy.

For now, our main task is to understand that currently we are on a wrong course; that under this regime the Azerbaijani people have no future; that each and every one of us, aware of our responsibility to ourselves, to our mothers, fathers, children, brothers and sisters and coming generations, must think and decide what needs to be done to take our motherland out of this crisis and save her from collapse.

INTRODUCTION

When the event inevitable cometh to pass
Then will no soul entertain falsehood
concerning its coming.

Koran, Sura 56

In the windy fall of 1990, the entire city of Baku was throbbing with rage. It was the devastating rage of the people who had had it with slavery. And so we came to topple the statues of idols – the Baku Commissars – chiseled in granite and marble.

Soon after the events of October 1917, the Bolsheviks started provoking interethnic conflicts at the periphery of the empire in order to seize power. The Baku Commissars were no exception. Led by Stepan Shaumyan, Lenin's loyal disciple, and devoured by ethnic hatred, in two months they executed over 100,000 Azerbaijanis, thus laying the foundation for installing a Soviet regime of fear and terror.

Paradoxically, the monuments to these Bolshevik terrorists who destroyed the national elite and 20 percent of the population were erected by the orders of the Azerbaijani Communist Party without any directives from Moscow. The totalitarian regime forced people to greet with applause the unveiling of monuments to the revolutionary idols whose etched faces were as a rule distorted in rage and hatred. It was a true act of blasphemy that people were forced to applaud the graven images of those who murdered their ancestors.

Once the people were free to show their real feelings toward these blood-soaked bandits, they instantly knocked the Twenty-Six Baku Commissars off their pedestals.

Then came the turn for other idols. In early January of 1991 we removed Sergei Kirov from his bronze pedestal. This loyal soldier of the bloody revolution, this satrap and Joseph Stalin's closest comrade-in-arms, always eager to follow the despot's cruelest orders, Kirov, too, had been destroyed by the system, after he had worked hard to sacrifice so many innocent lives on its altar.

Clad in heavy boots and commissar mufti, his full round belly held by a wide military belt, he was nervously crumpling a visored hat (an imitation of Stalin's) in his left hand; while his right hand, cutting through the air, was pointing forward. Or perhaps upward; it was hard to tell.

All these little Lenins and Stalins and many other bloody idols – large and small, sculpted in clay, granite, and bronze – all had their arms stretched out. It was part of their posture, as they showed the way to the abyss. Like a goat that leads a herd to the edge of the cliff, they led the crowds to the abyss, into which everyone was pushed, guilty or not. They did not bother keeping score of their victims; all they saw ahead was a mirage of the bright future. And it was in the name of this future that they were committing crimes on the national scale.

The idols made the rules for the crowds, while they lived lives of absolute monarchs. They developed and implemented an elegant theory of a labor camp, a monstrous reservation that embraced a whole population, including its creators, who in time would become the inmates and victims of the rulers who would succeed them.

Back then, our task was to topple the idol whose statue, occupying the high ground, had dominated the city for years. The workers of the factory where I was the director, my friends and fellow thinkers – we had been waiting for this moment for a long time.

I remember an old Azerbaijan movie, where a character asks: " *Vay*, Allah, when will you remove this scarecrow hanging over our heads?" By the filmmakers' design, he was a bad guy, naturally.

Only a year or two earlier we could not even dream of such a turn of events.

The people were sending the idols en masse to the scrap heap of history.

So finally the day came, with a chilly Baku wind, when a crane operator barreled up Hill Park and had the bronze sculpture grabbed by its armpits. But the stubborn idol put up a fight, and took a whole three days to uproot. The monument seemed to be writhing in mortal agony, and in that it was like the whole system that was grabbing at straws to prolong this agony for a few more moments.

Eventually, all that was left of the monument was a pair of rough soldier boots with metal rods sticking out. The boots remained on the pedestal for some time, but finally they crumbled, too, under the harsh Baku winds, which created an empty square-shaped lot.

A young foreman who stood at my side on that memorable evening asked me: "Rasul-*muellim*, can it be that one day they'll place another idol on this lot? Haven't we had enough?"

For all of us, the days of 1989 were the dawning of a new, genuine democracy. All of us – students, workers, farmers, engineers, professors – felt that no power in the world could suppress our desire to be free. We inhaled this freedom with such dizzying joy, with such admiration and sense of victory – no one could foresee the black January of 1990, filled with the treachery of Kremlin evil spirits, with cruelty and disregard for morality, typical of those who reach for power at all costs.

But most of the horrors still lay ahead, and we were still drunk with freedom. We considered ourselves already free, and were therefore madly happy. But the darkness was moving in with steely inevitability. The dark forces were testing freedom for sturdiness.

For Azerbaijan, 1989 was a year when the entire people rose against the Communist regime, against the Soviet Empire. The next year, 1990, was a year of ordeals, when the collapsing machine of the empire tried to suppress the democracy in our country and thus undermine the resistance in all Soviet colonies.

As I write this, I wonder: what is it that forces me to pick at the scabs of those years? Should one be surprised that evil and treason have befallen all eras and all nations? What's so new about what I'm trying to say?

But I do think I have something to say. Moreover, I am obliged to say it.

At least two reasons have forced me to pick up a pen.

First, today I am certain that, as we face the 21st century, we can clearly see the global problem of our planet, of our common dwelling where many have to live on top of one another, as they used to in standard Soviet housing. It is the problem of the Man of Planet Earth as a carrier of our civilization's greatest achievements through generations.

The universal nature of this problem renders absurd any attempt to prove the superiority of any culture, religion, nation, a group of people, or a clan – regardless of their contribution to the development of a given country or region. Einstein's relativity theory, Shakespeare's *Hamlet*, Tchaikovsky's Sixth Symphony, and Van Gogh's paintings are as dear and close to me, a citizen of Azerbaijan, as are Gobustan cave murals or soul-gripping songs of our singer Bul-Bul. I perceive all of it as my intellectual property that carries no proscription, no sign that would prevent other strangers from using this most precious and mobile form of estate.

The ideas of democracy, the concepts of an open society, that have been developed through centuries and undergone every ordeal, must be also included among great achievements of human culture. It does not take an outstanding politician or economist to perceive and appreciate the ideas and concepts of democracy. This form of existence of a man of reason is so necessary and inevitable that I perceive the great democratic principles arrived at by the United States and other civilized countries as my own life principles. Once I, or anyone else who cannot and will not be a slave, have partaken of these principles, no torture will force me to concede the desire and opportunity to live free.

For both an individual and a society as a whole, democracy is a universal as well as a unique form of existence of mankind, as long as mankind follows nature's great design – the propagation of human life on earth. Just as the variety of life-forms on earth made it possible for Homo sapiens to emerge and prosper, coexistence of people with various ideas and concepts is an essential form of life of a society that is not historically doomed. Devotion to a single ideology and a single manner of coexistence transforms human society into a military barrack, whose doomed existence is based on dogmas of lies and fear. This is what caused the fall of the Evil Empire, a hypocritical state that abhorred the variety of its inhabitants' ideas. The creators of the first – and, thankfully, the last – Socialist labor camp knew this very well. They deliberately created situations where fear was the only force to secure social cohesion. It was fear for one's own life, but even to a greater degree, fear for one's family.

There is a highly typical episode in Soviet history. It has been documented, first by Russian writer Soloukhin, that in the very first years of the Revolution, Lenin deliberately created famine in Moscow and St. Petersburg. His objective was to amass all bread in the hands of the State and then use it as both the stick and the carrot. A professor of philosophy, a farmer, a priest, the so-called food dictatorship would force equal obedience on all of them. But the primary target was gagging the intelligentsia, since, when it is hungry, it becomes silent and eager to please the feeding hand.

According to Lenin, "the objective of the Communist Party is to take the tired masses looking for a way out, and lead them down the path of labor discipline, where rallies about working conditions [obviously, the workers were still resisting] will be coordinated with total obedience to the Soviet director, a dictator where work is concerned. Submission, especially total submission to the directives of Soviet executives, whether elected or appointed, and furnished with dictatorial mandate."

These dictators, elected and appointed with unlimited mandate, have been poisoning our hearts and minds for decades. They were united by one thing: hatred for their own people.

The words used by the Orthodox Church's Patriarch Tikhon in addressing the "leader of the workers of the world" in 1918 sound like a collective curse on all Soviet and post-Soviet dictators:

> It does not matter what name you embellish your evil acts with. Murder, violence, robbery will always remain sins. They are crimes crying out for revenge. You promised freedom; freedom is a great good, if one perceives it as freedom from evil and freedom from oppression. But you did not give us this freedom. You have used your powers to persecute your brothers and to destroy the innocent. This is the truth: you have given the people stones, not loaves; snakes, not fishes. The prophets' words

have come true: 'Thy feet tread on evil and hurry to shed the blood of the innocent; thy ideas are unjust, and your path leads to death and harm.

Let me tell you a popular anecdote about Stalin.

One day the dictator comes to visit his mother. Once a laundress, she now lives in a small room in the mansion built under the Czar for his viceroy in the Caucasus. The ailing mother cold-shouldered her son who, ignoring her will, had dropped out of the seminary. She berated him with folksy simplicity:

"I heard you keep an entire people in fear and famine. Why do you need that? Have mercy on the people. You're one of them, too."

Iosif left in silence, and then came back, holding a tiny clump of dry grass, and with a herd of hungry bleating lambs. The lambs regarded their leader with awe and admiration as each tried to have a larger bite of grass than others. Then Stalin ordered that the lambs be fed with fragrant hay and other lamb's delicacies. Once the herd had their fill, they wandered away, ignoring their leader.

"See, Mom," he finally addressed his mother, "a lamb loves you when it is hungry and afraid. You feed it, it forgets who the boss is. That's how our people are, too. I wish them no evil. I just want them to live in love and peace."

They say that in real life he did not visit his mother, Keke, much; but according to his biographer, Edvard Radzinsky, such a meeting did take place in 1935. Allegedly, the son asked his mother why she had beat him so hard when he was a child.

32

Maiden's Tower, Symbol of Baku.

History Chronicled in a Carpet.

Ancient Manuscripts.

Azerbaijani Carpets.

Teardrops of Kyapyaz by Sattar Bukhlulzade.

Gobustan Cave Murals.

Geokchai Pomergranates by Togrul Narimbekov.

The old, infirm Keke said, "This is how you turned out to be a good person." Then she asked him what he had become.

Without false modesty, Stalin said, "Remember the Czar? Well, I'm kind of like a Czar now."

Actually, he was more than a czar. The Czar could not even dream of the privileges that the leader of the international proletariat bestowed on himself.

Like all subsequent Soviet dictators, Stalin was at best a mere worthy disciple and follower of Lenin's cause. It was Lenin who had formulated the theory and the practice of a state of slaves and executioners, who from time to time trade roles. All of these dictators were unanimous in their methods of reaching the state of total obedience. Either they create artificial famine, or provoke domestic or foreign danger, or, finally, stage conspiracies. Each of these methods is designed to immobilize the crowd and render it obedient and prone to manipulation.

I am certain that neither mob instinct, nor sheeplike solidarity with leaders, nor the desire to conceal your individuality in a chorus of exaltation – none of these qualities is characteristic of Homo sapiens. Naturally, barrackslike methods of ensuring obedience may succeed temporarily in effecting order and stability, but such order and stability are an illusion, fraught with risks of excessive disorder and disaster.

This concept has been confirmed at all times by various dictators, whether they were smart or stupid, kind or cruel, vicious or moral. The dictator's departure, inevitable as life and death, always turns into a tragedy for the nation, the state, and individuals. There

are no exceptions. Lenin, Stalin, Mao, Tito, Mobutu...
The list of names is long, and they all have something
in common. Each bespeaks a tragedy erupting after
the name appeared in an obituary. And then the seemingly accepted march of time is disrupted, and the seemingly eternal truths lie in ruins.

The reason for this is that a dictatorship prevents a
person from expressing his individuality, his uniqueness, in the face of tradition and principles, whether
freely evolved or imposed from above. A human being expresses himself not through slavish humiliation
and submission, but through free expression, through
a desire to improve his lot: this is his nature and true
essence.

By saying this I am trying to underscore my thought:
democracy is a natural necessity of a man's life, agree-
ing with his nature and designation. Totalitarianism,
dictatorship, tyranny stand for an unnatural, antilife
condition and inevitably lead to a catastrophe.

Democratic principles developed by human civilization through centuries are the source of great wealth
and constitute an intellectual property for all of us.
Everyone has an equal right to use it, and there is no
question who is more worthy and who is less worthy.
Belonging to mankind is the only license one needs.

Let me try to formulate the second reason for writ-
ing this book.

There is a term in chemistry: *limiting stage.*

The following phenomenon is observed: in a mul-
tistage sequential process, the general rate of progress
and tempo of the entire system is determined by this
limiting stage – the most conservative, the slowest one

34

– no matter how fast the rates of all the preceding or succeeding stages can be. No matter what you do, this is the stage that both determines and limits the general progress.

In my mind, this analogy applies to human society. Despite the extraordinary achievements in science, technology, and culture in countries like the United States, Japan, Germany, and others, the general pace of world civilization is slowed down by the processes taking place in any country that has traded one form of totalitarianism for another. Not only is each of these countries at the crossroads of geopolitical progress, affecting events in other regions, but it also represents a certain historical juncture by affecting the tenor and conscience of the entire world. Often, contrary to the logic of global, large-scale events, it is such distress areas that cause the most sudden turnarounds in world history as a whole. What we have here is a reversal of cause and effect: sooner or later, under the powerful influence of global civilization, a backward nondemocratic country is bound to take the path of truly democratic development. At the same time, civilized countries cannot – have no right to – remain indifferent to these local ulcers that affect the entire body of earth. Such indifference is not only immoral; it is pernicious for the entire civilization.

The brightest, most refined authors, the true aristocrats of the soul, the ones who rejected the Bolshevism from the first moment they saw its vices, or left it after their illusions had vanished – they had a well-defined foresight of the pernicious consequences of the most hypocritical system in human history.

Ivan Bunin, who, while in exile, won the 1933 Nobel Prize in Literature, wrote as early as 1924 on the occasion of death of the Revolutionary Idol No.1:

How do you gain power over the crowd, how do you get famous through Tyre and Gomorrah, how do you take over the former Czar's palace, or at least get crowned as the champion of people's commonweal? You must fool the crowd, and sometimes yourself, too, your own conscience; you must buy the crowd's favors by cajoling it. And so we have whole hordes of heralds of "new" life, who have gained a global privilege, a license to arrange for the highest human good – allegedly distributed in universal and equal fashion. We have a whole army of professionals, thousands of members of various social parties, thousands of orators, some of whom eventually attain prominence. But, I repeat, you cannot achieve all that without a Great Lie, a Great Cajoling, without creating disorders and revolutions, without an occasional trek through blood up to your knees. But the most important thing is to deprive the crowd of the "opium of religion," to give them an idol, a calf – or, simply put, cattle. Pugachev, the 18th century Russian peasant rebel! What could he do? "Global" cattle are another matter. At the height of his activity, a bastard like Lenin, a moral cretin from birth, could stun the world with monstrosity: he laid to ruin the greatest country and slew several million people. And yet the world is so insane as to argue, still: was he a benefactor of humanity or not?

The experiment in building a society devoid of property and responsibility ended in a disaster, after taking away millions of lives. The intelligentsia were affected the worst of all, despite the pleading of Maxim Gorky, the founder of Socialist literature: "You must not beat up on the intelligentsia, gentlemen – these are the brains of the country, its most valuable treasure!" Bunin remarked:

> While Lenin and Dzerzhinsky were grinning: "Too late, pal! We have already beaten these brains out of hundreds of thousands of skulls! We have poisoned the world with our very existence, with the pus of impudence, savagery, shamelessness, lies – by now this moralizing about the value of brains is nothing but ridiculous."

The great Azerbaijani writer and philosopher Hussein Javid, destroyed by the Soviets for his devotion to the history and values of his people, created a unique character of *Iblis*, or Satan, which embodies the totalitarian rulers of all times and nations. Here he is, the ubiquitous phantom of evil:

> Iblis! How striking the greatness of your name!
> Your glory spreads through all lands in all tongues.
> In every house dwells Iblis, in palace and hovel!
> Iblis in ka'aba, in prayer-house, in taverns!
> All listen to me, though they may despise me.
> All obey me, though they may hate me.

But the humble fool who insults me:
You shall be punished, you unworthy.
Stamped out by my foot, you'll shrink,
And die out, wasted under my shoe.
But ye must know, ye have other rulers beside me....

Who is Iblis, then?
– Treachery itself.
Who is a man who sells everyone at once?
          – Iblis...

In Siberia, Javid's grave is marked by a simple birch cross with a number. His executioners thought they were using the cross to hammer the very notion of freedom and self-expression into the permafrost ground.

But cruelty only resulted in greater resistance, displayed by people labeled as dissidents. They started the system on its path to ruin.

Many of them naively thought that the reason for the system's failure lay in certain deviations from the basic principles of society of universal prosperity and justice. Others called for and admitted a possibility of convergence, of a peculiar merger between capitalism and socialism. Both notions were equally illusory.

There is no, nor has there ever been, "Communism with a Human Face": even in theory, its creators called for blood and violence.

In my opinion, the champions of convergence erred in the following way: when comparing two opposite systems – one represented by the United States and other civilized countries and one represented by the Soviet Union and its satellites – they assumed, for "simplicity's sake," that the United States was a capitalist country (according to classical Marxist definition of distribution of means of production) and the Soviet Union were a Socialist country (according to the same definition). In reality, we were dealing with a different pair of opposites: on the one hand, an open democratic society with its problems and opportunities, evolving according to the specific trends of the open market, and, on the other hand, a closed totalitarian society, where natural human and social laws and needs were replaced by the will of a dictator, or, at best, a dictatorial junta.

If the first model is an evolutionary one, i.e., developing in accordance with natural objective laws, the second is a revolutionary one, i.e., changing in accordance with a subjectively written scenario and held together by the fear and obedience of the population.

While the first system develops and improves itself in an ascending curve, the second one is preserved solely through artificially created social conflicts, such as the slogan of heightening social conflict, or cultural revolution, or development of virgin lands, etc. How can one argue a convergence of an open and a closed system? Rather, one would arrive at the conclusion that there is a possibility (or a natural outcome) of the second system being absorbed into or transformed by the first one.

To be perfectly sincere, the most effective and genuine explanation for the spontaneous breakup of the Soviet Union (which, contrary to Marxist-Leninist theory, took place without a Capitalist v. Socialist apocalypse) lies, in my mind, in the opening of the East-West curtain. Once we saw the reality and wondered why everything this side of the curtain is worse in quality and lower in number (except, perhaps, the number of nails per capita), the artificial system called Socialism started deteriorating from inside. By now, I believe this is clear to everyone, and in the first place to us, the guinea pigs in the most horrible experiment in history.

It is also clear to me today that we, the Azerbaijanis, just as the rest of the humanity, possess enough historical, psychological, and moral worth, that our children and the following generations should live in an open democratic society, according to civilized laws, with every individual enjoying freedom of thought and a right to choose.

I believe that this eye-opening process that has been so long in coming is inevitable. And we can only bow our heads in gratitude to those whose eyes opened to it before ours did. I think that Sura 94 of the *Koran* puts it best:

Have we not
Expanded thee thy breast?

And removed from thee
Thy burden

The which did gall
Thy back?–

And raised high the esteem
[in which] thou [art held]?

So, verily,
With every difficulty,
There is relief.

Verily, with every difficulty,
There is relief.

40

Chapter One

AZERBAIJAN: THE LAND AND THE PEOPLE

1. WE, THE AZERBAIJANIS

According to the *Koran*, the Moslems' holy book, the first people were Adam and Eve. And Allah said to Adam: "Let thee and thy wife settle in paradise and eat... wherever you please, but do not approach this tree."

In other words, this legend follows others almost verbatim: the Flood, the punishment of Sodom and Gomorrah, and so on. The differences from the Bible are minor, and historians provide some explanation: Mohammed, they say, learned not only from communicating with God directly, but also from the stories of merchants and priests, many of whom he had met while trading in Syria.

From a historical or ethnographic point of view, these borrowings from the Bible are not unusual: the commonality of Jewish and Arab legends stems from the same Semitic roots.

The mass conversion of Azerbaijanis to Islam, a progressive monotheist religion replacing the cult rituals of fire worshippers, goes back to the early 8th century. It started out in the towns in the deltas of the Kura and Araz rivers, on the Caspian shores, and on Mugan and Mil plains. Islam has become an inseparable part of world culture, and is the religion of over a billion people on all continents. Islam is the faith and the worldview of the Turkic peoples.

According to the Lev Goumilev, a prominent researcher of Turkish ethnic groups:

It is time to dot the i's in the issue of "inferiority" of peoples of the steppes and oppose the Eurocentric theory that regards the world as the barbarian periphery of Europe.

…Ethnology does not pose the question who is more cultured: Huns or Greeks, Turks or Germans. Ethnic groups can be cultured and creative today and turn to stagnation three hundred years later, while in another fifteen hundred years no one will know their name.

…Even at a glance – and we could peer more closely in order to find resemblance in detail – one cannot find a reason to consider the Huns inferior to Europeans, whether modern or ancient ones. Moreover, one has to give proper due to the intelligence and diplomatic tact of the Huns and the Turks. They treated neighboring ethnic groups as equals, however different from themselves. They never saw the world with themselves at the center and barbarians on the outskirts. And this is why, despite facing a stronger opponent, they won. Their key principle consisted not in slaying their neighbors

but holding on to their territory, their cultural
and historical traditions, their motherland...

Today, when we hear pretentious theories about the
relative importance of some ethnic groups vis-à-vis others, every intelligent – and, I dare say, decent – person
will agree with these notions. Today, one often reads or
hears about "greatness" or "global nature" of a certain
large nation, though sometimes these sentiments are
expressed by people with crossed eyes and protruding
cheekbones.

Azerbaijanian ethnos goes back to 3000 B.C. As a
single Turkic ethnos, it was formed under the influence of various historical "flows": there were raids
and large-scale invasions, tribe migrations caused by
geographic and climatic changes, as well as trade and
caravan routes, the most prominent of which was the
Great Silk Route. Each of these "resettlements" involved acquisition of new customs and rites, which
affected language, crafts, and culture.

Historically, Azerbaijan was a shelter of sorts for
people who sought peace and quiet and avoided both
raiding and being raided. Perhaps this led to such distinctive features of my people as a peaceful nature, refined hospitality, and respect for the guest regardless
of ethnicity or appearance. Even now, the poorest family welcomes a guest by setting the table with every bit
of food they have, making the best bed, and not bothering him with excessive questioning. I believe this tradition is almost genetic in nature: through our ancestors' experience, we subconsciously realize that a trav-
eler must replenish his strength and energy in order to
start a new life in a new place. Therefore, first he must

be made aware of kindness and have a glimmer of hope. This hospitality may well be the most typical feature of my people.

According to the map of disturbances suggested by Goumilev, Azerbaijan went through a series of historic "shocks":

(Beginning in the 18th century B.C.): Formation of Upper Egypt, the fall of the Middle Kingdom, the Hyksos conquest of Egypt and emergence of the New Kingdom, the Hyksos and Hittite military campaigns, the Hittite conquest of Asia Minor, and the conquest of Babylon.

(Beginning in the 8th century B.C.): Emergence of Roman military society, Roman conquest and formation of Italian Republic. Emergence of Samnites, Etruscans, Gauls, Hellenes, Lydians, Karians, and Kilikians, and later, Midians and Persians. Emergence of fire worship.

(Beginning in the 6th century A.D.): Emergence of Moslem Arabs, Islam, Arab expansion to Spain and Pamir. Emergence of two new ethnoses in Northern China: Chinese-Turkic (the Tabgaches) and Chinese Medieval. The fall of the Tabgachi Dynasty, the emergence of Koreans, formation of centralized state in Japan, the spread of Buddhism.

(Beginning in the 13th century): Expansion of the Lithuanian Duchy from the Baltic to the Black Sea, the adoption of Christianity, the rise of the Moscow Duchy, the intermingling of Slavic and Turkic populations of Eastern Europe, the emergence of Ottoman Turks, the consolidation of Moslem East with Janissaries and "sea tramps," the formation of military sultanates, the Ottoman conquest of the Balkans, Near Asia, and North Africa. The expansion of Ethiopian Christianity and Ethiopian Kingdom in East Africa.

To these global changes we could add the events of the past two centuries, especially the dynamic processes of the 20th century...

The formation of the Azerbaijani people and state took place under the influence of these global planetary waves lapping at our shores. The decisive role in the formation of our language is played both by the Turkic tribes who lived here in ancient times and by the Turkic tribes who settled here later.

The ancient Turks played a prominent part in world history: they brought together the cultures of China, Iran, Bysantium, and India. They left a deep trace in history, due to the nature of their society and "steppe" mentality.

An interesting historic fact should be mentioned. The transformation of the ancient Turkic Khaganate into a number of Turkic states was caused in part by deepening conflicts on its borders, in the steppes, and in the conquered lands. The conflicts were in turn caused by unreasonable taxes and levies.

Even in those days, Azerbaijani taxes were rather high: panning for gold, mining of silver and copper, fishing – all these were taxed, and taxes were collected according to a census. Current tax authorities should think, too, of the historically inevitable consequences of their rule...

Azerbaijani history abounds in prominent personalities who at different times attempted to introduce democratic changes that would take into account their own culture and that of other lands.

By no accident, the most progress was made under those statesmen who not only were young of age, but also carried new progressive ideas of their time and widely involved the best and the brightest in their rule.

Javanshir (616–686), who came to power at the age of 21, not only succeeded in liberating his country from Arab and Khazar invaders, but used flexible diplomacy to make peace with his neighbors, thus securing his people's independence and dynamic development of crafts, trade, and culture. He made his palace attractive to scientists, poets, architects, craftsmen, serving as their patron and at the same time seeking their advice while making important decisions.

Babek (798–838), who at the age of 18 headed the Khurramite movement against Arab invaders, brought together the warring Azerbaijani factions and created a highly professional, disciplined army, with cavalry playing a major part. His personal courage and nobility made it possible for him to use broad popular support in the war of liberation. He saw the strength of his state in popular unity and prosperity, and appointed the brightest persons to executive positions, deeming that they would place independence and national welfare above personal interests.

After the new Arab warrior Afshin Kavusun improved tactics and the organization of his army and dealt the Khurramites a number of defeats, the feudal warlords panicked and withdrew their troops from Babek's army, thus bringing his life to a tragic end.

Tempted by the reward placed by the Arabs on Babek's head, his former friend and comrade-in-arms Sakhl ibn Sumbat lured Babek and his family to his

46

palace and handed them over to the Arabs for 1,100,000 drachmas, a gem-studded belt, and a crown.

Another prominent statesman was Ismail Safavi, known in history as Shah Ismail (1487–1524). At 13, he headed the Kyzylbachi movement, and at 15 became the first Shah in the Safavid dynasty. He brought together the Turkic tribes: the Shamlus, the Rumlus, the Ustajulus, and many others. Clad in hats that featured twelfe red stripes and were wrapped in turbans, the Kyzylbachi sowed panic in the enemy ranks with their battle cry: "Oh, my teacher, my *murid*, may I give my life to him!"

Shah Ismail the First shaped nomadic tribes into regular troops and, beginning with the summer of 1499, went on a campaign of uniting Azerbaijani lands. He brought together the lands of Naxcivan, Ardebil, Shemakha, Asia Minor, Baku, South Azerbaijan, and Tebriz. In the fourteen years of his rule the Shah conquered many provinces, including Khorasan, Iran, parts of Turkmenistan, and southwestern Afghanistan.

Ismail had himself crowned as the Shah of Iran, starting the tradition of Azerbaijanis as Iranian monarchs. He announced Azerbaijani the official language and made his court a magnet for the most talented poets, thinkers, and scientists, who formed a sort of State Council for developing the most acceptable and equitable state decisions. As a poet, he became known under the name of Khatai, and he made a contribution to early Turkic-Azerbaijani literature, leaving behind a number of poetic works and philosophical tracts. As many other talented poets, he died relatively young – at 37 years of age.

Perhaps the most democratic government in Azerbaijani history was formed on May 28, 1918, after the fall of the Russian Empire and was led by Fatalikhan Khoysky. Consisting of bright individuals (Mukhammed Gasan bek Gadji, Nasib bek Yusifbeyly, Khudadat bek Melikaslanov, Mamed-aga Shakhtakhtinsky, Democratic Party leader M.Rasulzade, and others), it represented wide social strata and intended to join the international community, following the standards set by civilized states. Not only did it acknowledge existing international agreements, but it was also creating the modern social infrastructure, putting education at the head of its agenda.

The intellectuals who joined the government realized that the true wealth of a nation is determined by the level of its intellectual life and education system, as well as the understanding of the economical base of a democratic state. The Azerbaijani Democratic Republic lasted less than two years, but even in that short time it opened a university, numerous schools, and sent its most talented youths to study in the best schools of Europe and America, their tuition paid by the government and philanthropists.

Unlike Lenin's Bolsheviks, whose slogan was "Rob the robbers," Azerbaijani Democrats respected property rights and the right of a citizen to acquire wealth through labor and intellectual effort. Those who decided to destroy "the old world" and build the barracks of military communism could not abide that. Thus, on April 27, 1920, the only genuine Azerbaijani democracy was drowned in blood. The invading barbarians acted deliberately: first, they executed and exiled the industrialists and intellectuals to make it easier to soliloquize about a "happy future". These builders of "the new world" killed 99 percent of the Azerbaijani intelligentsia. Terror went on for decades, and even those who managed to escape abroad were assassinated – for example, Fatalikhan Khoysky, the government's first Prime Minister. Many other Azerbaijani democrats were subsequently shot or poisoned, including Nariman Narimanov.

Cries for help remained unheard; the "civilized world" decided not to get involved. The West adopted a wait-and-see attitude. This would recur time and again...

Like many other countries, Azerbaijan retains traces of our prehistoric ancestors. Remnants of *Azykhantrop*, a Neanderthal man, dated over 450,000 years old, were found in the Azykh cave, not far from Fuzuli, a town barbarously destroyed during the 1988–97 Armenian military intervention.

There are also numerous remnants of fortresses in Azerbaijan, attesting to various historical events on its territory. Its northern border was defended by the Derbent Fortress, situated on the Djalgan Ridge of the Caucasus. The ridge ends about three kilometers from the Caspian Sea and turns into a narrow passage, called Hun Pass or Khazar Gate. The fortress itself, called *Demirgapy Derbent* for its cast-iron gate, served to protect the land in ancient and medieval times. It changed hands repeatedly, which is reflected in a number of inscriptions. From the Islamic period, there are inscriptions of Pakhlavi and Khazars; the Shirvanshah period left traces in the form of sophisticated architectural details; and the early Middle Ages are represented by simple heavy symbols.

The construction of the Derbent defense system was finished by the end of the 7th century, following the construction of Gilgichai and Beshbarmak systems, dated as early as the 3rd century. Taken together, these were designated to defend Shirvan.

By the 18th century, Panakhali Khan had completed Askeran Fortress *(Askeran Galasy)* in order to defend Karabakh. He also built the city fortress of Shusha, which he planned to call Panakhabad. It was thought that no foe, no matter how strong, could conquer the fortress by assault – an earthquake was the only danger. Alas, in those days treachery was not taken into account.

Also impressive are the city fortresses of Shiz, called Gendjek in pre-Islamic times and situated in the Afshar Region of South Azerbaijan. Shiz was a religious center and served as a treasury location for two pre-Islamic empires of East Asia: the Parthians (8th century B.C.) and the Sassanids (3rd–8th centuries A.D.).

Natural defenses were important, too: mountain ridges with numerous cliffs and valleys, among which the most prominent are Kerogly-galasy, Gyz-galasy, and Gyaur-galasy. Kerogly-galasy was named after Kerogly, the great defender of freedom and human dignity, and the protector of Azerbaijan regions from Magrib to Mashrig.

Gyz-galasy, or the Gyulistan Fortress, still carries traces of the 9th century. It was the last refuge of Shirvanshahs, and protected Shirvan in the Middle Ages from Arabs, Seljuks, Mongols, and Ottomans. It is associated with names of such statesmen as Manuchekhr, Akhsitan, Halilluakh, and others.

Edifices of Peri Gala, or Virgin Fortresses, considered to be a Zoroastrian temple, still remain in the village of Yukhary Chardaglar. The Gyaur Gala fortress in Nakhchevan dates back to 2000 B.C. and has much in common with Hittite fortresses. The banks of the Arax River are dense with fortifications. The most famous here is the fortress of Alinjah, allegedly admired by Tamerlane himself.

Other ancient castles and towers on the Azerbaijani territory include Adjine Tepe (10–11 centuries B.C.) near the village of Gasanlu and Sary Tepe (4 or 5 centuries B.C.) in Kazakh Region.

Beginning with the 12th century, the Caspian shore at Absheron was fortified against pirates' raids. Castles and towers were built in Mardakyan, Shuvelyan, Buzovny, Bilgya, and further inland in Kaly, Mashtaga, Ramana, Fatman, Balajary, Amiradjan, Sabunchi, Kishly. The castle of Bailov was built as a sturdy fortress, on the foundation of an even more ancient one, but fell during the earthquake of 1306.

One of Sheik Shamil's captains, Sultan Daniel-bek, built the fortress of Sumug in the village of Ilisu, Kazakh Region. Together with Chinghiz and Sheytan towers in Zakataly, it is a historical monument as well.

This abundance of fortresses shows that reliable defense has been a major concern, though it did not always work.

The Azerbaijani language, a worthy member of the Turkic language family, which formed through a 2,000-year history, is the native tongue of the Azerbaijani people, adopted both by ancient ethnic groups and

51

by later ones. Uniquely, it started out as a commoners' language, and later replaced Arabic and Farsi as a literary one, in which many prominent literary works were written. Modern Azerbaijani culture is an amalgam of many others: Sumer-Accadian, Assyrian-Babylonian, Hittite-Mitanni, Urartian, Mede-Iranian, Greco-Roman, Byzantine, Arab-Moslem, Scythian, Turkic, and many others.

Under the Communist regime, the Azerbaijani language was often a target of the Kremlin's most servile lackeys. Some did not like the presence of Arabic words, others wanted to get rid of Farsi terms, while yet others attacked Turkish borrowings. They truly tormented our language, repeatedly changing the alphabet and executing the most talented writers and poets. The bureaucracy developed its own tongue, the lingo of apparatchiks, marked by its abundance of consonants, especially the sound of "*r.*" Words like "*parrrty,*" "*dirrrective,*" "*prrrovocation,*" came from their mouths like a dog's bark.

Still, the language evolved, despite their arbitrary orders and edicts. It absorbed words that fit its melody and rhythm, becoming richer and more democratic, and it could not be ruled by edict. The charm and naturalness of the Azerbaijani language come from its truly popular nature; as a rule, people get rid of the chaff, and accept only what is close to their hearts.

I would say that the Azerbaijani language, democratic in form and euphonious in sound, is the most powerful weapon of our people. Armies may surrender and retreat, but the Azerbaijani language does not surrender and is not for sale. The language of my people is a national hero as much as the legendary Kerogly or Babek. Rather than erecting statues to the fly-by-night leaders, I would put up a bronze monument to the nation's most faithful soldier – its language.

2. OUR CONTRIBUTION TO WORLD CIVILIZATION

At Expo '67 in Montreal, the pavilion of Israel had a most unusual display. It did not have samples of electronics or biotechnology. Instead, a thousand pictures were suspended at various levels under a dome, representing Jewish people who made a contribution to sciences, arts, and philosophy. This was more than enough to show the meaningfulness of a nation on the global scale.

Naturally, I cannot cite a thousand prominent Azerbaijanis within one short chapter. But even a few examples should give the reader an idea of the uniqueness of my people's contribution to mankind's culture. My choices may be subjective, but perhaps this makes it easier for me to reproduce a fraction of what has been achieved by Azerbaijanis.

The great poet Nizami lived and wrote in Gyandja in the 12th century. While the capital of Shemakha was ruled by Shirvanshahs, who were courted by obsequious poets and fortunetellers, Gyandja was ruled by viceroys, appointed by Atabeks. Their power was unstable, and the town was the scene of constant battles among Georgian kings, Atabeks, Turkic Kipchaks, and Shirvanshahs.

Gyandjans were famous for their courage and tenacity. Once they refused to surrender to the Georgian king and claimed they would submit only to Shirvanshah Abu Bekir. Later, too, they show the same qualities in other conflicts, but often they will fall victim to less fierce kings and self-appointed crown-seekers.

Perhaps it was this special situation of Gyandja that made Nizami treat his characters carefully, without drawing distinction between craftsmen and kings. To him, human nature, emotional depth, and intelligence came first; the social standing of the person was secondary. This gained Nizami prominence among Azerbaijani poets of all times. Even the most talented of them never shunned royal favors, for which they paid with exalted odes. Nizami stood above these natural weaknesses; to him, the rulers were characters in a stage show, with himself acting as both a director and a writer. At least no one could reproach him that he had ever been untrue to himself and sold out his talent.

His main concerns were the mystery of the human soul and the relations between words and deeds. But his main character was a person in love, for to him love was not only the source of passion, but also a great stimulus of constructive activity. His characters love and suffer for their love for longer than a fleeting moment. Their feelings undergo grave ordeals, and therefore lead to great feats. Their love is not a casual spark, but an ongoing bonfire, and the poet follows it from the moment the first woodchip catches fire through wild flames to barely perceptible smoldering.

Nizami's favorite poet was his contemporary Hagani Shirvani, who, though he lived at the Shaheenshahs' court, exclaimed in his famous *Divan*:

> The kings' palaces are like the sea
> With hundreds of sharks
> And not a single pearl,
> And they'll take away your soul...

In the same critical essay Hagani defined the purpose of his existence:

> A man must serve his society
> Like soap,
> Which, though vanishing itself,
> Makes itself useful to people.

For the poet's sharp tongue and refusal to flatter, Shirvanshah Akhsitan kept Hagani for eight months in the Shabran jail. In contrast, Nizami did not have to tear himself apart between the truth and serving the rulers.

Nizami was well versed in classical sciences and philosophy and was familiar with Thales, Plato, Socrates, and Aristotle. He rose to such a level of philosophical thought that even now, at the threshold of the 21st century, we perceive him as our contemporary. Among the heroes of his historical poems were not only Alexander the Great, Darius, and Aristotle, but common merchants, builders, craftsmen, shepherds, and other working people. He treats them all with the same love and compassion, for life is short and desires are infinite.

Nizami widely used legends, especially in his famous *Iskender-name*, an epic poem about Alexander the Great's campaigns, where the king is accompanied by Aristotle and other sages.

Barely has Alexander taken the throne when he is being told of a need for military action: friendly Egypt has been attacked by the army of King Palangar, the ruler of Zanzibar. Following his vizier's advice, Alexander embarks at the head of an army of his most courageous and experienced soldiers.

The battle has been joined: horsemen clash, swords clang, blood flows. Dead-tired soldiers, without having dealt the other side a decisive blow, retire for the night. Early in the morning, Alexander sends Palangar his emissary Tutiyangush to propose that Palangar surrender, for Alexander is fierce and ruthless, and his soldiers are invincible. In full view of his own soldiers and the Greeks accompanying the emissary, enraged Palangar stabs Tutiyangush. Blood spurts out of the wound; Palangar pours it into a glass and drinks it in one gulp. Panicked Greeks return to Alexander's camp and tell him the horrific story of cruel bloodthirsty Africans.

Desperate, Alexander turns for advice to Aristotle, his tutor, who inspired the emperor to embark on the warpath:

> Up, he said; 'tis time to test your lot.
> It is an honor to strike down this kind of beast.
> When your soldiers gain victory,
> This will secure your kingdom.

Now, Aristotle gives the young emperor wise and practical advice: your troops cannot conceal their fear, and, in order to conquer it, you must do something that would impress both your army and the foe even more than Palangar's blood-drinking.

Alexander acts promptly. With his soldiers watching, he personally beheads a prisoner and tells his chef to cook his head. After a while, the wise chef returns, but instead of the prisoner's head he brings the head of a black sheep, stewed in herbs. The emperor lustily polishes off the stew in full view of his soldiers and African prisoners, who take this to be a cannibalistic ritual.

Terrified prisoners, allowed to escape, return to their king to tell him of the meal. This demoralizes Alexander's foes, while the Greeks, on the contrary, are enthused: their leader is even more feral and bloodthirsty. Naturally, Alexander wins the battle, having personally felled several African strongmen and their leader Palangar.

> The King sees: no end to trophies.
> As if an ocean of sand has leaked into the desert.
> ...The King is glad to have both the triumph
> And the trophies; sadness and despair are forgotten.
> Yet he glances at the abundance of victims
> And, though smiling, in secret his soul filled with blood.
> Why in just one battle so many people
> Were slain with swords and poisoned arrows?

The depth of Nizami's vision is striking. In the Middle Ages, it was standard for a poet to glorify warriors and rulers, to extol their victories, to enjoy their attention and tender mercies. But Nizami values human life more highly; he perceives sacrifice in the name of trophies and conquered lands as meaningless. Unlike Hagani, he believes that, like any other laborer, the poet must serve the common good, which is to stay alive, rather than sacrificing itself.

To me, this reveals the great humanism of his philosophy. A man who willingly takes the path of self-sacrifice – a samurai, if you will – is fanatically intolerant and ruthless toward those who are unlike him and who do not fit his notion of truth. Xenophobia is a destructive force. One wishes the champions of "pure nationalism" would understand this simple truth and draw a bitter lesson from the past, when espousing this philosophy led to nothing but victims and self-devourment. Nowadays, all too often these "samurai" lead desperate crowds and vanish in the decisive moment. As they lead others to death, they never consider their own mortality.

To me and many of my contemporaries, Nizami revealed the truth about such eternal human notions as love, loyalty, faithfulness, etc. Before we read Shakespeare, we were already familiar with Leila and Medjnun, Khosrov and Shirin; but we never perceived Nizami's characters as perfect, idealized stick figures. They were as weak as we; their souls could soar and fail. Despair led them to rash deeds, for which destiny punished them cruelly. And that, too, is the truth of life.

Through his characters, Nizami inculcated in us respect for courage and disdain for treachery. However, we did not get to test these qualities in real life until much later, and it turned out to be much harder than we believed in our youthful imagination.

I believe that the unique nature of Azerbaijan poetry stems from the unique nature of its language: musical, soft, rich in imagery. An Azerbaijani phrase is like a mountain stream: you remember it the way you do a melody, like a lyric from a favorite song. You just cannot pronounce it indifferently. A concept comprising several phrases is like a musical carpet: sound is generated by a combination of colors and lines. It contains nothing excessive, nothing alien; once that appears, you can immediately sense falseness and incoherence. I would say that a complete phrase uttered in Azerbaijani is like a crystal grown under meticulous conditions.

Perhaps this is the reason why almost every phrase uttered by Azerbaijani writers and poets enters everyday language. Whether Azerbaijanis are holding business negotiations or just chatting at a feast, they are apt to quote extensively from their prose and poetry, so that a phrase uttered on the most trivial occasion sometimes reflects an entire work of literature. Perhaps it is related to the above-mentioned feature of the language: it was born among common people and later became a tool for great wordsmiths. It is so very Azerbaijani to be enamored of the word, of their poets and writers. We possess an organic need to express ourselves in the same phrases used by the characters of Khagani, Nizami, Fizuli, Vagif, Nasimi, Khatai, Mirza Shafi Vazekh, Natavan, Sabir, Jalil Mamedkulizade, Mikail Mushfig, Gusein Djavid, Samed Vurgun, Rasul Rzy, Ordubadi, and others. Many of them perished tragically under Stalinist repressions, as did many other Soviet intellectuals.

Manuscripts of Nizami's works are held in the British Museum, and UNESCO celebrates Azerbaijan's brilliant poet and philosopher in its anniversaries.

To me, Nizami soars above time and space, addressing the past and the future in equal measure, fully remaining our contemporary.

A similar attitude to life and the world is typical of a contemporary of mine, an artist named Sattar

Bakhlulzade, who lived in the second half of our century. Sattar was a follower of Favorsky, a famous pre-Revolutionary Russian graphic artist, and became known to Azerbaijani people as an artist who cherished the beauty and poetry of his native land. The land was everything to him: his mother, his beloved, and the source of his passions and feelings.

In order to tell the truth, Nizami left his reality for ancient times. Sattar followed a different path: he left modern society for nature, the primary source of all things.

He borrowed extensively from the philosophy of Fizuli, who lived in the early 16th century and had followed in the footsteps of Nasimi, another remarkable poet, in creating Azerbaijani literary language. Fizuli had to coin Azerbaijani words and expressions on the basis of official Farsi, and sometimes, in his own words, he "used Farsi as a thread to put in a pearl, for which I picked the fruit of my heart off a branch."

As Sattar learned, Fizuli had discovered the main mystery of true art: one should depict only what an artist's soul perceives. Only then will the poet's word be accepted as the truth, for such a word is a sign that goes back to the creator himself. And then the artist becomes the conductor of the truth coming from God. Otherwise, it is Satan that moves his heart and his hand.

To Sattar, it was no accident that Fizuli's work is contemporary with *Kitabi Dede Gorgud* ("My Grandfather Gorgud's Book"), the great Turkic epic, which seemed to comprise history in nonstop battles, where the best and the worst of mankind came to the fore. Sattar turned to the epic as well, using it as inspiration.

At that time, the epic was practically forbidden. One of the reasons was Stalin's dislike of the Azerbaijanis. He wanted to exterminate our nation, the way he tried to do the Chechens. His Satanic plot was under way: both before and after the war, whole villages of Azerbaijanis were exiled to Siberia and Central Asia in cattle cars, which were unloaded amid deserted steppes or taiga forests, in the hope that the exiles would die of severe cold and famine. Yet the nation survived.

Sattar was lucky to have copied the almost complete text of *Dede Gorgud* in Arabic. He knew it practically by heart, but was especially fond of its leitmotif:

> Where are the beks, the sages
> Who claimed that the world belongs to them alone?
> Taken by death, concealed by the earth –
> So whose is now this mortal world?
> Hey, the coming and the leaving world!
> Hey, the mortal world of the last finale!

In these words, he discovered the comparison of two elements: the eternal good and light that come from God, and the mortal evil that accompanies the endless battle for power in the world. The artist devoted himself to one element only: the fairy-tale purity of nature.

Most of Sattar's paintings are landscapes dedicated to specific Azerbaijani locales, which are reflected in the titles: *Tiny Tears of Kyapyaz, A Nakhchivan Landscape, A Caspian Beauty, An Azerbaijan Fairy Tale, The Land of Fire*, and others.

Sattar's view of the world was that of a man enamored of life and beauty. He seemed to ignore the flaws, the wounds, the boils, caused by the men who followed the Soviet biologist Michurin's words: "We should not expect favors from nature. Our task is to obtain them by force." And so the insane man kept "obtaining," or rather stealing, everything that was not nailed down, so to speak. He was leaving behind entire fields of oil residue, poisoned the atmosphere with noxious gases, and dumped mercury and sulfites into the Caspian. The man was deprived of his function of a master and proprietor, and he turned into a parasite, sometimes into a burglar and a rapist; while the land – nature – was always the victim. Sattar wanted to see the land in its pure form, unmarred by human excesses; he wanted it to remain dazzling, magical, hospitable, offering its gifts of its own accord.

His paintings are all of a piece. They make a striking impression by means of an entire ensemble of colors, which seem to create a sound with lyrical hues. The remarkable unity of the depicted items turns his paintings into picturesque symphonies; it seems that the sound is built into the brushwork, and the painting exudes it along with the light. Sattar found the divine in a green sprig, in a reflection on the water's serene surface, in the luxurious blossoming of field poppies and cornflowers. He never tired of being amazed at nature's extraordinary harmony of form, color, and sound, which always led him to think of the Superior Mind – the Creator. For him, nature was the source of purification, of ablution, of touching the truth. And he had a wonderful gift to convey this emotion with his paints. He seemed to take us away from our dry, vicious reality to the world of harmony and pure thoughts.

I know of no other artist who believed so convincingly in the perfection of this world, despite the all-too-obvious chaos and deviations from morality.

What seemed like Sattar's self-removal from public events, from political intrigue, caused more than mere misunderstanding and misperception; it brought him vicious hatred of the powers that be. He was "discovered" for "internal use" very late, practically toward the end of his life. They disdained him because he came to official receptions wearing a simple working jacket that belonged to a relative, who actually worked at an oilfield. He was never invited to feasts, because he eyed the elite like a dervish and never uttered the cliches about the Party and the Government. He preferred to quote Fizuli or the *Koran*.

Every time I walk into a room with his paintings, I feel as if I were in a temple, where everything is meant to worship a remarkably natural, harmonious world, a world that predisposes the viewer to calm, unhurried perception of truth, and the true meaning of existence. He is not in a hurry to enjoy beauty; he prolongs this great enjoyment and allows us to come along.

Sattar left behind his lightest icons, his fables of Azerbaijan nature, so that in the bleakest moments of our history we could pause and decide: this is the limit. Beyond this lies the end of the legend and, perhaps, the end of life.

Next to Sattar, or some following him, stand such unique, colorful painters as Tair Salakhov, Togrul Narimanbekov, Rasim Babayev, and others, for whom the joy and the pain of the earth constitute the essence of art and existence. Today, their works are displayed in the Tretyakov Gallery and the Russian Museum, and many foreign collections. Assembled together, they have a lot to say about our land and its people; most importantly, they inspire and preserve hope.

I would also like to share my experience of one of the most remarkable Azerbaijanis, Zia Bunyatov, a scientist and an academician, who dedicated his life to recovering the pages of Azerbaijani history that were concealed or banned through the criminal design of rulers big and small.

Bunyatov experienced every possible ordeal of life in the Soviet Union. As a young man, he commanded a special "penal" battalion in World War II, risked death on many occasions, went through all major battles from the Caucasus to Eastern Europe, and was awarded the title of Hero of the Soviet Union. But in the time of peace, too, he was a man of tremendous courage, which he combined with the qualities of a fine research scientist. It seemed as if he never ceased to command that battalion. He had to fight through the defenses of silence and lies erected around the history of Azerbaijan. Occasionally, he fought single-handedly while everyone else was watching from the sidelines, expecting him to stumble.

The cause of his life was Azerbaijani history and proving that Azerbaijanis are members of a large family of Turkic-language ethnic groups. Together with his followers – Sarah Ashurbeili, Yusuf Yusufov, and others – he proved that Turkic tribes have lived on the territory of modern Azerbaijan since ancient times, and that this factor was decisive in the formation of the Azerbaijani language and ethnos.

Bunyatov started by studying economic development in the Bronze Age and then moved on to specific periods: 7th to 9th centuries, the time of Atarbeks, and early 20th century. He knew his material in depth and could not be fooled, though the Soviet historians repeatedly tried to falsify the historical truth.

Zia Bunyatov was in the forefront of events during the memorable days of popular unrest in Baku and other regions. He addressed million-strong crowds outside the House of Soviets with inflaming speeches, and the crowd absorbed his every word. People knew he was telling the truth. And his way of telling the truth was a direct one. His style was of the warrior and scientist.

He was a big man, both literally and metaphorically, and those for whom his truth, rough and unpolished, stood in the way found him a convenient target. He was assassinated for his inability and unwillingness to remain silent. He was killed mercilessly: after stabbing him many times, they fired a final shot in his mouth, as if to shut him up for everything he had said and would still say. His murder is a spot on the conscience of all the dark, hateful forces, and a continuation of Stalinist terror that did not spare anyone who had his own opinion.

To me, academician Bunyatov was a scientist and an enemy of compromise, for whom there was no other criterion but the truth of life.

In my opinion, a special feature of the best Azerbaijani scientists is their desire to bridge the gap between the abstract world and reality, between the past and the future, by means of philosophical rethinking of the essence of being. Here I should mention the great scientist and philosopher Nasir ad-Din Tusi (1201–1274); naturalist and science popularizer Zardabi; Yusif Mamedaliyev, the first President of the Azerbaijani Science Academy, who helped research in petrochemistry and implemented many discoveries in industrial alkylation and photochemical chlorination; academician Murtuz Nagiyev, one of the creators of the recycling theory, which is the basis for many industrial processes; Professor Vezir-zade, who developed theory and practice of mineral crystallography; academician Azad Mizadjanzade, who applied the concept of non-Newtonian media to the behavior of oil in strata; and many others whose names are known all over the world.

My portrait gallery is far from complete. There are composers: Uzeir Gajibekov, Muslim Magomayev, Kara Karayev, Fikret Amirov, Arif Melikov, and Niyazi. There are performers: Shovket Alekperova, Rubaba Muradova, Sara Gadimova, Khan Shushinsky, Bul-Bul, Gurban Primov, folk bard Alesker, Rashid Beybutov, Muslim Magomayev, Abil Kyaman, and many others, loved and esteemed by people.

But I have to stress one creative entity: the Azerbaijani people. They are the ones who invented a colorful musical language with unique forms – _bayat, tesnif, rast, seygah_ – and lyrical, dynamic dances. Their hands created carpets striking in form and color: _palas, yeyim, kilim, zil, sumakh,_ as well as the refined lines of chalices, ladles, trays, belts, and daggers made of copper, bronze, silver. Finally, we cannot omit their sincere and respectful hospitality and generosity.

3. Our Potential Future Contribuctions and the Obstaclles in Our Path

As a country, Azerbaijan possesses unique natural qualities.

Its territory is 86,600 square kilometers in the middle of the Caucasus. In the south and southwest, it borders on Iran (611-km-long border) and Turkey (9 km). In the west, it borders on Armenia (566 km) and Georgia (322 km). In the north, it borders on Russia (284 km). Finally, its eastern border with Russia and Central Asian countries runs along the Caspian Sea. Nakhchivan Autonomous Region is separated from Azerbaijan by a strip of Armenian territory, while inside the republic we have Nagorny Karabakh Autonomous Region, which has been the site of tragic events of the last eight years.

Azerbaijan houses nine climate zones, from Lenkoran 's subtropics to the snowy peaks of Shahbuz and mountain fortresses of Kerogly-galasy, Gyz-galasy, and Gyour-galasy.

In creating Azerbaijan, God was generous and inventive.

Lenkoran area grows rice, tangerines, lemons, and tea. Nakhchivan: walnuts and apricots. Shemakha and Djalilabad: grapes. Geokchai: pomegranates. Karabakh: mulberry trees, figs, pears, apples, cherries, plums. And all over the place, persimmon and almonds, dates and pine cones, melons and watermelons, mushrooms, berries, and medicinal herbs. So generous is Azerbaijan nature.

Its land holds deposits of oil, gas, polymetal ores, nonferrous and noble metals, precious and semiprecious minerals, construction rock, mineral and thermal waters – everything you need for all branches of the economy.

Another precious asset of Azerbaijan is the sea, with sturgeon and crab and even eel, with salt and iodine and bromide compounds, and sea-bottom oil of the highest quality.

Possibilities for tourism and archeology are numerous: holy places of fire worshipers; Gobustan, a unique ancient settlement with cave murals; Binagady, burial ground of birds and animals; prehistoric settlements in Nakhchivan and Karabakh; fortresses and castles and ancient temples and unique burial sites of Zoroastrians.

There are possibilities that are totally fantastic from the point of view of modern medicine: treatment of cardiovascular, rheumatic, and other conditions at Dary-dag hot springs, Naftalan oil, mud baths, medicinal herbs, radon mines...

Such is the potential of my land that can be turned to everybody's benefit, if nature is treated carefully and gently.

How has it been treated all these years?

The land of Azerbaijan was raped and destroyed by brainless, immoral politicians and managers. It was drained of anything that could bring instant reward without any regard for tomorrow.

The Party ruled: at first the lands, traditionally farmed for grain, were turned over to corn, then cotton, then grape vines. Then the Party changed its mind again, and vineyards were cut down. An outsider might conclude that madness seized the land, perhaps in the anticipation of apocalypse. On the receiving end of this madness were peasants, who were trusted only to voice their loyalty to their "benefactors" and kiss the hands of "comrades" who then decided to call themselves "misters".

Sumqayit Chemical Works, Kirovobad Aluminum Factory, Baku industrial plants – all these poisoned the land for years to come. So much rhetoric was heard about Sumqayit being a "living implementation of Lenin's ideas" and aluminum factories being "symbols of technological progress."

In fact, all the industrial projects built in Azerbaijan during the Soviet years are examples of failed and extremely dangerous technology without any degree of environmental protection.

Let me draw this picture. For decades, the Caspian Sea has been the dumping ground for industrial waste, mineral and organic acids, mercury, inorganic substances that included practically the entire table of periodic elements, organic solvents, dyes, tars, powders. The air was polluted by every kind of hydrocarbon from methane to hexane; chlorine, carbon monoxide, the noxious dust of compounds of fluoride, chlorine, aluminum, chrome, and sulfur. Finally, tanneries added to this horrific cocktail, making its consequences irreversible.

Consider the waste from oil industry alone: altogether, over 1 billion tons were produced between 1848 and 1980. Of these, about a quarter, i.e., 300 to 400 million tons, were dumped into the Caspian as raw oil (between 1848 and 1925) or heavy oil products (1925 to 1950) or as a complex mix of industrial waste (later years).

The Soviet planned economy put crippled nature in a concentration camp, turning human beings into uncaring slaves and rapists.

Today, the Azerbaijan environment is in a state of crisis.

The rest of the country's life – economy, science, health system, sports, culture – is in a similar shape.

How could this happen? How could a rich, healthy land be turned into a sick patient? The organism's defensive mechanisms are lost, and "ideological" principles, good for short-term deception, no longer work. What is the agenda behind dooming the greatest national wealth – its intelligentsia, who have already been destroyed once – to extinction or emigration?

The fall of the empire after a long period of stagnation was caused by numerous objective and subjective factors. An important role was played by democratic movements in the former republics, which waged national-liberation struggle. Along with Baltic lands and others, Azerbaijan was in the forefront of that struggle. Our movement had broad popular participation, and the Kremlin's efforts to preserve the empire were destined to fail.

In Black January of 1990, in Baku, regular Army troops were ordered by Marshal Yazov, General Bakatin, and KGB executive Bobkov to attack the peaceful population with tanks, machine guns, and bayonets. Actually, the orders came from the Kremlin, from Gorbachev and Prime Minister Ryzhkov. (On a recent visit to Armenia, the latter proudly admitted that he had personally issued the order to send the troops in order to bolster Vezirov's puppet regime.) I would go further and say that the 1990 Baku events were one of the defining moments in the fall of the rotted-out superpower.

Once again: with its whole population participating courageously, Azerbaijan was in forefront of the struggle for the new democratic life. Up to a million people gathered on the square facing the House of Soviets and the cement sculpture of Lenin, the idol of bloody revolution. All ethnic groups were represented, all social layers, all ages. So monolithic was the unity that one felt: here is a genuinely democratic movement, it must bring us victory. There was no doubt; victory seemed at hand. Power, order, structures, resources, will, intellect – the people seemed to have it all.

What prevented us from creating an open democratic society? What prevents us today from joining the civilized world?

If we tackle this issue objectively, which is no easy task for someone who directly participated in these events, we should admit there is a whole set of reasons, both domestic and foreign. Here are the most important ones:

First of all, the democratic forces lacked a common political and economical platform, which led to the split of the democratic front, who had brought the former regime to collapse.

This is the sequence of events in Azerbaijan preceding and following the breakup of the Soviet Union: By 1990, due to efforts of all groups of the population, the democratic movement is rising. Azerbaijan becomes one of the hotbeds of unrest in the Union. The movement is spearheaded by the Popular Front. Baku and other cities resound with mass protests against the Kremlin's tyranny.

January 1990 sees provocations from the republic's Party leaders, punitive troops entering Baku, and massacres of peaceful population. The movement intensifies. The Kremlin's puppet Vezirov is overthrown and replaced by another one, Mutalibov. Many leaders and activists of the Popular Front are arrested.

Preparation for presidential elections is going on during the state of emergency. The democratic movement is losing momentum. Beginning in July, as the election campaign nears, the conflicts between the Front's leaders widen. Some of them sell out people's interests and accept Mutalibov's offer to share the power.

September 1990: the elections. In contrast to the democratic elections in Russia and Baltic countries, the ones in Azerbaijan are completely controlled by Ayaz Mutalibov. The democratic movement loses ground. Several of its leaders, forsaking democratic principles, conspire to share power with Mutalibov.

Early 1991 sees a staged presidential election. As a political leader, President Mutalibov shows complete ineffectualness. Once again, the strategy and the tactics of the Party leadership are rehashed, with the most trivial questions resolved in the center of power.

The August coup in Moscow. Mutalibov's contemptible tactics are aimed at reviving the power of the Party and the KGB. Despite favorable conditions, democratic forces are unable to take power. Contrary to the logic of events, Ayaz Mutalibov arrives at power by "egitimate means" and follows it with a farcical presidential election in September 1991.

Yet the government has no program or objectives of its own, and concentrates its efforts on propping itself by creating terrorist military units like "Gardashlyg."

With Mutalibov's regime discredited, the Popular Front comes to power. The Kremlin's viceroy flees the country.

Thus, the Popular Front won an easy victory over its opponent who had neither a well-defined program of action nor a capability to resolve political and economical issues. It would seem that now they should reinforce democracy, create competent government, and move toward an open society. Instead, "democrats" appoint their own regional "ittle czars" from the least competent, most power-hungry cadre, create "black beret" military units, and, instead of solving political and economical issues, wage internecine demagogical debates. Their disdain of professionals and intellectuals leads to a situation where all the legislative acts of the Azerbaijani Parliament, which still consists of Party nomenklatura, are essentially translations of acts of the Russian Parliament.

As a result of incompetence, amateurishness, ignorance of politics and economics of a democratic state, the Popular Front suffers a debacle. This takes place against the background of economic chaos, military defeats, destruction of science and education, and the stoppage of almost all industries and agriculture.

Similar, or quasi-similar, situations exist in other former republics, where former Party leaders, who know how to spin palace intrigue and delude the population, come to power. With a complete lack of ideology, and with total political and economic incompetence, these people know how to take advantage of chaos.

With former republics lacking formal democratic infrastructure, with political and economic issues being resolved by old-fashioned centralist methods, with no competent professionals and public forces involved in decision-making, the populations of these countries are doomed to impoverishment, both economically and spiritually.

The power vacuum, the impotence and incompetence of newfangled dictators, lead to higher dependence on external factors, such as superpower pressure. Social destabilization is a result of the West's indifference, its wait-and-see attitude toward the problem of creating open democratic societies in the newly independent states. Such a strategy on the part of the civilized society could be justified if the time factor had not been so dangerous and would not lead to the most unpredictable consequences.

In the case of Azerbaijan, the situation is complicated by Nagorny - Karabakh. Let me touch briefly on the nature of the military conflict in this region of Azerbaijan.

Nagorny-Karabakh Autonomous Region is situated inside the country, in the southwestern part of the Caucasus Minor. Its territory is 4,392 sq.km.; its dimensions are, north to south, 120 km, and east-west, 35–60 km. It comprises five administrative districts with the capital in Stepanakert (a Soviet name that replaced the ancient one of Khankendi). Before the events of 1988, its population was 170,000, of which the Armenians numbered 123,000 and Azerbaijanis, 40,000. There were also representatives of 40 other ethnic groups.

Despite its small size, the region comprises three different climate zones, with plentiful mountains and rivers such as Terter, Indjachai, Khachinchai, Karkarchai, Kendelenchai, and Kuruchai. It has such mineral deposits as lead, zinc, and copper in the form of sulfide polymetallic ores. There are also deposits of construction materials: marble, lime, fireproof clay. The area of Shusha has the Narzan ferrocarbonic mineral springs.

The local population formed through intermixing of old tribes with various newcomers. As a result of the Turkmenchai treaty ending the Russian-Turkish and Russian-Iranian wars of the 19th century, Armenian families from Iran and Turkey were resettled in the area. Altogether, over 130,000 Armenians were resettled in various areas of the Caucasus in those years. According to the Russian poet and diplomat Alexander Griboyedov, who represented Russia at the negotiations, "The Armenians were mostly resettled on Moslem landholders' estates." He also mentioned the need to impress "upon the Moslems that the current difficulties are short-term, and they should not be concerned about the Armenians taking permanent possession of the lands they have been allowed to stay on."

After the formation of the USSR, Nagorny-Karabakh as an administrative unit was included in Azerbaijan.

The problem of drawing territorial boundaries in the former Soviet Union is a more extensive subject. One thing is clear: the manner in which they were drawn was meant to complicate and render mutually contradictory the states' mutual claims at their slightest attempt to become independent. This principle was followed without exception in all former republics, and was a key factor in the explosion of national conflicts when independent states were formed.

This holds for the Caucasus as well. Mutual interpenetration of ethnic groups in Georgia, Armenia, and Azerbaijan is a historical phenomenon. Before the described tragic events, Azerbaijanis were driven from Armenia, where 400,000 of them used to reside. The events of 1988–90 were not unique: earlier, in the 1920s, over 1,200,000 Azerbaijanis lived in the territory of Armenia, and they were repeatedly driven from their traditional areas of residence. Approximately 400,000 Azerbaijanis reside in the Georgian territory. Similarly, up to 300,000 Armenians used to live in the territory of Azerbaijan. At the time of the formation of the USSR, the area of Zangezur, which had always been populated solely by Azerbaijanis, was "cut off" and handed over to Armenia.

Nationalist conflicts started in 1980, with the Kremlin looking the other way. Its rulers regarded these conflicts as another reason for military intervention aimed at suppressing democratic movements in the republics. Thus the conflicts grew into explosive situations in several areas of the USSR.

In Nagorny-Karabakh, the Kremlin played the card of a separatist movement demanding separation from Azerbaijan. If initially the activists talked about reunification with Armenia, which is the genuine objective of separatists, later, in order to pass it off as a national liberation movement, they formally demanded an independent state. Russian politicians have used the situation in order to put pressure on Azerbaijan, which, like the Baltic countries, embarked on the path of autonomous democratic development without getting involved in the military and political intrigues of the former metropolis. This is the root of the military conflict between Armenia and Azerbaijan on Azerbaijan's territory. These are the results: Azerbaijan's military defeat; Armenian annexation of over 20 percent of Azerbaijan's territory, including the towns of Kubatly, Zangelan, Kelbajar, Agdam and adjoining villages, Shusha, Lachin, and Khodjaly. This created over one million refugees – women, children, old people – from the territory.

Refugees on the territory of their own state.

A horrifying paradox of the late 20th century.

One can assess the results of this bloody war in different ways. Who won? Who lost? Who profited, financially and politically, from the war? The answers to these questions will bring us close to the truth.

In order not to be misunderstood, let me quote from an independent disinterested source. Mark Shteynberg, a retired colonel of the Soviet Army now living in New York, outlined his version of these events in *Novoye Russkoye Slovo*, a Russian-language New York newspaper. Mr. Shteynberg's view is not comprehensive, yet there is much in his conclusions that reflects the truth.

He cites the following data regarding the materiel of the former Trans-Caucasian Military Zone:

4th and 7th General Armies, 19th Air Force Army, 19th Anti-Air Defense Army, Caspian

Navy, and Poti Naval Group of the Black Sea Navy. After the breakup of the USSR, according to the Tashkent treaty of May 15, 1992, each Trans-Caucasian republic was entitled to 220 tanks and as many armored vehicles, 285 artillery systems, 100 war planes, and 50 attack helicopters.

The quoted balance of armaments was temporary. First there were rumors, and then, at a Duma session, General Lev Rokhlin quoted the numbers pertaining to the "commercial deal" between Armenia and the Russian military.

The Armenians "bought" 8 R-17 tactical rocket complexes, 27 Krug anti-aircraft launch systems, 50 BMP-2 armored vehicles, 18 Grad jet artillery systems, 306 machine guns, 7,910 automatic weapons, 1,847 handguns, over a million shells and rockets, and 230 million bullets. The total sum of this order exceeded 1 billion dollars, with the client paying only for transportation. In other words, Armenians got it all gratis.

The Russian Government had an interest in this country's successful waging of the war and eventual victory over Azerbaijan.

General Lebed, a former presidential candidate who had seen military action in Baku, Afghanistan, and Moldavia, recently visited Karabakh troops, and was impressed: "I haven't seen such a well-trained military unit in a long time."

I cannot help sharing a very simple thought regarding certain elements of the Russian military. I am talking about the ones who think along the lines developed by Joseph Stalin and use a "corporal"-level concept of victory: If we take this hill, this means we have won. The number of the dead and wounded is irrelevant. This has happened many times in the Soviet history: you down the glass – hundred grams of pure alcohol – you sniff your sleeve instead of a chaser, and – forward march to your death. The fatalities are built in and are not counted. This is how it was in the wars with Finland, Germany, Japan; and it was repeated in Afghanistan, in Chechnya and Moldova. In none of these massacres did the Russian generals spare the lives of their soldiers. The objective was always the same: take the hill at any cost. On the other hand, a human life was never valued in that system. The price was known only to the soldiers' mothers and wives.

I suspect that up to this day many generals still have not learned why they are neither loved nor respected. They performed their duty in Azerbaijan, Georgia, the Baltics, and Afghanistan through bare yelling and curses. It was too hard to use their brains and try to understand the aspirations of those whom they trampled with tanks and pierced with bayonets. Understanding was not required.

Summing up the status quo, Shteynberg writes:

Unfortunately, these wars cannot be considered completed. The leaders and nations of Trans-Caucasus are in no way content with the results, and the mood of revenge is all over the place from the Black Sea to the Caspian. This is why, instead of focusing on the stabilization and reconstruction of the economy, substantial resources are being spent on strengthening the armed forces and preparation for the future bloodshed.

As I mentioned earlier, this account contains some truth. However, it is missing some aspects that affect the general tone of the evaluation.

Throughout my career as the Speaker of the Azerbaijani Parliament I have directly participated in the efforts to resolve the conflict – in meeting with representatives of Armenia and Karabakh and in many other ways. I will not go into the detail of the military conflict – much of it will be clarified in due time – but today I wish to stress the following:

The war in Nagorny-Karabakh did not start out as a national-liberation movement of an enslaved or an oppressed people. Moreover, despite appearances, it was not even a war between the people of Armenia and Azerbaijan. This war was initiated as a dirty, bloody, and immoral game by political adventurists from many sides. It was a political and economical operation, a distracting action on the part of those unable and unwilling to embark on the path of democracy. It is a deal made by blackguards who continue to benefit from it even as it continues to take innocent lives.

However, the conflict transformed itself into a war of liberation for the Azerbaijani side. A million people are left without shelter and have been deprived of land that has been in families for generations. A million people, young and old, have lost the property that had been earned and inherited. There is no second opinion: the war and tensions will persist until the occupied territories are returned, one way or another. I pray God that the peaceful path, with the participation of civilized countries, prevails.

None of this is a secret to the leaders who play parts of peacemakers and fathers of their nations. In time, justice will be rendered to each of them. For now, negotiations are being waged, gestures made, soliloquies uttered. For now, a million people are trying to solve the problem of shelter, work, existence – unable to forget that they have been driven away from their land.

The wars in Karabakh, Chechnya, and Abkhazia have their screenwriters and directors. The latter sold their souls to the devil long ago, and each of them is branded with the mark of the beast created by the Maker – whether by error or by oversight.

Whatever the case may be, common people do not need this war. It is a boon only to those who invented it, implemented it, and continue to play it as a trump.

I think – I am certain – that reason and the hearts of Karabakh residents will bring peace to this land. Like God, Truth is one, and it consists in a simple notion: the meaning of human life lies in perpetuating it, rather than destroying it. Each dead Azerbaijani or Armenian is a dead dream and hope, a ruined life of children, mothers, and wives.

Bertrand Russell appealed: "Let us preserve our respect for truth, for beauty, for the ideal of perfection that life prevents us from achieving. Let us learn the energy of destiny that allows us to live with a constant vision of the good. Let us stoop in our deeds to the world of real facts that contains this vision."

81

Chapter Two

CLOSED SOCIETY AND TOTALITARIANISM

1. FROM PLATO'S *REPUBLIC* TO STALIN'S EMPIRE

Throughout the past twenty centuries human society has developed in accordance with two basic concepts originally proposed and elaborated by ancient Greek philosophers and politicians, first and foremost Plato and Pericles.

Pericles maintained that all members of society should be able to and are entitled to judge, though only selected persons are capable implementing the judgement.

Plato, on the contrary, argued that the absolute obeisance of citizens to one leader is the highest social principle. "One should get up, or move, or wash, or take his meals... only if he has been told to do so. In a word, he should teach his soul, by long habit, never to dream of acting independently, and to become utterly incapable of it."

In my mind, the most revealing and precise definitions of the foundations of open v. closed, or totalitarian v. democratic, societies were provided by Sir Karl

Popper, an authority on Greek and modern philosophy. I did not turn to Popper by accident. Joseph Kraft, an American observer, wrote that "no thinking person would be doing himself a service by neglecting Popper's book."

My fascination with Popper went beyond his brilliant and highly original analysis of ancient Greek philosophers, the founding fathers of Western civilization; beyond the London University professor's impeccable judgments and categorical conclusions; finally, beyond his exciting plot with dazzling and convincing conclusions. For me personally (and for others, I suspect), the main distinguishing feature of Popper's book, *The Open Society and Its Enemies*, is that it approaches the story of Plato and Socrates not merely as an archeological study that suddenly reveals new interpretations, but as an event highly relevant to the world today.

That was his original idea: to reveal basic, somewhat idealized models of open and closed societies, so that even a passing glance would suffice to show the stark contrast between the two. Popper removes the wrapping and focuses on the main aspects that define the two models' fundamental essence. In the process, the models become deliberately "simplified" and theoretical in a sense, yet this approach helps evaluate modern social phenomena more reliably.

Popper does not fail to admire the Greek philosophers as great thinkers and perceptive students of human relations, yet in his assessment of their conclusions he does not make allowances for their reputations. He focuses on one substantial aspect: is it the man for the state, or the state for the man? When we approach one or another thinker or statesman, which of the two options does he develop? To Popper, the rest is just persiflage and special effects aimed at drawing the spectators to the performance that is Society. This approach fits in with the book's objectives. According to Bertrand Russell, Popper's book is "a work of first-class importance which ought to be read widely for its masterly criticism of the enemies of democracy, both modern and ancient."

Having analyzed Plato's political program, Popper concluded that the latter's basic demands are reduced to two formulas. The first, "Down with any political change," refers to idealistic notions of dynamic changes and state of peace; the second one, "Back to nature," reflects his natural-philosophy ideas. Popper places these two demands at the root of Plato's entire political program: division of society into distinct classes; the determining role of the ruling class; the ruling class's monopoly on various amenities; strict censorship prohibiting any changes in education, legislation, or religion; and satisfaction of economic needs as the state's main objective.

All these totalitarian ideas are developed against the background of ideas of Good and Beauty, Justice and History, of involving the wisest philosophers in ruling the state, of supreme happiness and purity for all citizens.

Nonetheless, Plato's program is fundamentally totalitarian. To Plato, "just" is what responds to the interests of the best state possible, i.e., whatever precludes fundamental change and preserves the social structure with the ruling class or group. In this state, each must do the kind of work that corresponds to his natural abilities: the ruler rules, the worker works, the slave serves. Justice is not defined by the nature of relations between individual citizens; nor, to Plato, does it consist in the state's equal treatment of its individual members. Rather, justice belongs to the state and is founded on the relations between classes. If the state is healthy, strong, and unified, then it is just and stable.

Popper draws the fundamental distinction between the humanitarian theory of justice (open society) and the principles of a totalitarian state (closed society). The former presumes equal treatment of all citizens without taking into account privileges, the general principle of individualism, and the defense of citizens' freedom by the state. The latter suggests various groups' and persons' entitlement to privileged treatment, the general principle of collectivism, and strengthening of the state through the efforts of every citizen.

Juxtaposing an individual and the state, Plato writes that "the part exists for the sake of the whole, but the whole does not exist for the sake of the part... You are created for the sake of the whole and not the whole for the sake of you." In other words, whoever is unable to sacrifice his interests for those of the collective is an egotist. The humanitarian point of view suggests the following pairs of opposites: individualism v. collectivism, and egotism v. altruism.

According to Popper, the combination of individualism and altruism became the foundation of Western morals, and the ethnic doctrine of Western civilization. To Plato, individualism presented a danger, as it could undermine the basis of the "perfect" state of his dreams. In such a state, he wrote, all citizens see, hear, and act in such a manner, it is as if their eyes, ears, and hands did not belong to them, but were the communal property. In such a society, people rejoice and get angry for the same reasons and at the same time. "And all the laws are improved for the purpose of the state's maximal unity." All the citizens, animals included, should be in a constant and comprehensive state of mobilization in order to maintain overall discipline, and the highest principle and the condition of stability consists in the absolute submission to the leader, devoid of any willfulness. Any display of anarchy shall be nipped in the bud; this lack of submission is punishable not only in people but in animals as well.

However one interprets Plato's ideas, one cannot escape sensing that he was pathologically opposed to any display of individualism and changes in society. Plato's moral code consists of collectivism and political utilitarianism. The highest moral criterion is the extent to which a given individual action benefits the state as a whole. Only that which is good for the group – the tribe – the state – can be good.

Thus, Plato's ideas are beneficial from the point of view of totalitarian, or collectivist, ethics. Citizens' deeds are termed virtuous if they are aimed at enhancing the state's military power; if they correspond to the state's tasks in form, effectiveness, and depth; and if they are committed at the right time and the right place.

Plato and his followers are sincere in their dedication to totalitarianism as they pursue what they see as the ultimate idea: the idea of the Good that leads to the stability and power of the State. Whatever promotes that ideal is justified.

At the same time the rulers are allowed to use any techniques and measures in order to maintain public order and state stability. These include totalitarian deception of both friends and foes. Plato says, "It is the business of the ruler of the city, if it is anybody's, to tell lies, deceiving both its enemies and its own citizens for the benefit of the city; and no one else may touch this privilege.... If the ruler catches anyone else in a lie... then he will punish him for introducing a practice which injures and endangers the city."

Such lies represent, first of all, the propaganda aimed not only at those governed by the wise and enlightened ruler, but at the ruler himself who must ultimately believe his own lie if it is aimed at strengthening the existing order and the state.

The utilitarian principle applies to the way the sick and the infirm are treated. According to Plato, the citizens of a stable state should not have time for being sick and getting treatment, while the doctors should not pay attention to and take care of those citizens who can no longer perform their duties, for such a person is useless both to himself and to the state.

In his book, Karl Popper vividly defines both open and closed societies, or, rather, their hypothetical models. A closed society, whose citizens' actions are subordinated solely to the prosperity of the collectivist state, is likened to a herd or a tribe with semiorganic unity and semibiological links. These are reflected in communal living, joint effort, common perils, joy, and grief. Such a society is a practical case for the so-called biological or organic theory that views the state as an organism, whose individual elements are assigned certain biological functions, with no change in places and roles allowed among these elements. Just like legs cannot function as a brain, obedient citizens of a closed totalitarian society cannot perform the functions of their leaders.

Popper views the extreme model of an open society as an "abstract society," which is to a certain degree devoid of properties of a specific group of people or a system made of such groups. An extreme state of such a model is a hypothetical society where people are occupied with their problems and, for practical purposes, have no personal communication. The communication takes place through modern technological methods. Such a society is completely depersonalized. Undoubtedly, this model is purely hypothetical, and the actual social condition is defined by closeness to the model.

The real-life open society features interpersonal relations of a nature fundamentally different from that of a closed society. Spiritually based relations predominate, while an individual's dependence on the state mechanisms is weakened. Each individual is given an opportunity to express himself freely within the framework of the reasonable rules of community of free people.

In other words, a closed society presumes that people live and work in the name of strengthening and stabilizing the state machine, whereas the essence of the open society consists in the free development of individuals protected by the state.

The basic difference between the two is reflected in the issue of state leadership. The closed society poses the question, "Who should govern the country (city, region, economy)?" In the open society the question is formulated, "How do we organize and improve our political institutions to make sure that an incompetent leader does as little damage as possible?"

The leadership qualities in the closed society were precisely formulated by Niccolo Machiavelli, who gained historical notoriety reflected in the word "Machiavellian," which stands for the ultimate degree of lack of principle in politics.

If one has gained power by criminal ways, Machiavelli advises that he destroy both his rivals and his most respected supporters right away, thus preventing the usurpation of power. A tyrant must display cruelty only once, so that people could later forget the taste of pain and offense.

Rewards should be given out from time to time, so that they are received with utmost gratitude. However, a certain balance should be maintained; i.e., while remaining unloved, the ruler should not evoke hatred. Fear is compatible with the absence of hatred, and the tyrant can always avoid contempt as long as he does not make claims on his citizens' property and wives. Nonetheless, that is permissible, too, if done with sufficiently weighty reasoning and solid justification. One should not especially worry about one's reputation for cruelty when dealing with the army, for no army can be united and disciplined without such a reputation.

The tyrant should surround himself with competent loyal people, for society will find the tyrant wise if his court fits this requirement. Yet this attitude may change if his subordinates are helpless and ignorant.

There are three personality types: the first one understands things the way they are; the second receives gratefully that understood by others; the third neither understands nor is capable of understanding through the explanations of others. The first one is excellent, the second is good, and the third is useless.

The tyrant must promote talent, encourage the gifted, and honor those who succeeded in their areas. He should be prepared to reward anyone who improves his craft, and he should not distract these people from the craft in which they prosper, nor deter them from new starts through high taxes...

The reason why I am describing the totalitarian ideas of thinkers long gone is simple: to show that the face of tyranny has undergone little change in centuries. A modern tyrant may, if the place and the time demand, call himself a democrat, and even claim spiritual values of his own or another nation, but his essence remains the same as it was in the days of Plato or Machiavelli. Compared with modern tyrants, however, Machiavelli looks positively like a Social Democrat.

Nowadays, as we face the 21st century, we see the same old tricks: new tyrants and dictators of all kinds use loud slogans about protecting national interests to cover up their true agenda as they subordinate entire societies and each individual to the interests of their clan or a privileged group.

All Communist revolutions set forth the total destruction of moral and ethical values developed by mankind as their primary task, along with the physical liquidation of the carriers of these values: intelligentsia, property owners, and priests.

According to the Communist doctrine, a new life could be built only on the ruins of the old world. As the Communist anthem goes:

> We will destroy the world of violence
> To the bottom, and then
> We will build our own new world
> He who was nothing will become everything

These lyrics are far from symbolic; their import is quite real. That was the main trick of "building of Communism": to begin from zero, from the ruins, and then build a grand asylum, whose inmates would rejoice at every drop of water and a piece of bread. Reduced to this state, masses are easy to lead in any direction and term it as movement forward to planned objectives.

Perhaps Karl Marx's *Manifesto*, which opened with an ominous mystical phrase, *A phantom wanders through Europe – a phantom of Communism*, was the most specific document to sing paeans to Communist slavery.

This document presents openly, without embellishment, the ideas of destructive fanatics, who were mostly motivated by hatred and loathing of everything mankind had created in its centuries of progress.

Here is the main thesis of this vicious document that was slammed into our brains since schooldays: "The Communists consider it beneath themselves to conceal their views and goals. They declare openly that their ultimate ends can be achieved solely through overthrowing by force all the existing social relations. The proletariat has nothing to lose but its chains. And he will gain the entire world."

By naming class struggle as the main social force, Marx laid a theoretical foundation for construction of the new world on the ruins of the old one. The road to new life was mapped clearly: through the destruction of the civilized world to the creation of a dictatorship of the proletariat. And there were quite a few who were willing to rob and destroy.

As it was explained to us, Marxist teachings were understood, adopted, and implemented in the countries that were the weakest link in the chain of imperialism. Originally, Socialism triumphed in Russia and China.

Lenin acted in strict keeping with Marxist theory. Some of his slogans were pure demagogy; others struck fear and horror in the hearts of people.

There is his famous slogan: "You can become a Communist only after you enrich your memory with the knowledge of all the treasures created by mankind." It sounds highly ironic when one considers that in all stages of the Soviet state, most Party leaders were ill-educated and had barely made it past the literacy courses. Moreover, not a single Party leader had ever read a single Lenin article in its entirety; as for Marx's *Das Kapital,* he may have come as close as the cover. The same perhaps applies to most Party members, in both the leadership and rank-and-file. The slogan became even more nonsensical when juxtaposed with Lenin's maxim that the Soviet state will be led by a dishwasher woman...

Even prior to creating the totalitarian state, in his work *The State and the Revolution* Lenin wrote in reference to the coming catastrophe:

We do not know by what stages or what practical measures mankind will reach this superior goal, and we cannot know that. But it is important to conceive the lie of the standard bourgeois view of Socialism: that Socialism is something dead, set in stone, unchangeable. In truth, Socialism is only a starting point for rapid, genuine, truly popular progressive movement that involves first the majority of the population, and then the entire population, and takes place in all the areas of social and personal life.

This statement of Lenin's became a sort of a departing point for the party's subsequent activity at all stages of the country's political and economic life. Without bothering to make sense of its own insane ideas, without subjecting the projects promoted by con men to serious analysis, the Party dispatched millions of people to senseless construction projects, to reclaim the "virgin" lands, to build the dams that would turn rivers back in their tracks. Each time, so-called popular enthusiasm was carefully orchestrated from upstairs, implemented by local Party branches, and resulted in millions of tragedies and broken lives.

As early as 1927, the great helmsman of the Chinese Revolution, the loyal and tested disciple of Marx and Lenin (whom he knew perhaps from their pictures at best), Mao Zedong described a peasant rebellion in Changsha Province in his article *Is It Terrible or Is It Beautiful?* He crowed how the peasant revolution was sweeping aside both small and large property owners and remarked how the momentum brought out cries of alarm not only from the property owners but from the middle class and even from the revolutionary-minded people, aghast at chaos and cruelty.

"They shout, *How terrible!*" Mao remarks contemptuously. "Even people who are quite progressive say, *This may be terrible, but in a revolution it is inevitable.*"

In other words, no one can avoid the word *"terrible."* A great peasant mass rose to perform a historical mission, to destroy the feudal landowners, and in a few months they managed to achieve what they had failed to achieve in centuries. That is why, in Mao's opinion, so great a destructive achievement cannot be called "terrible." It was a magnificent sight to behold: huge crowds destroying their class enemies.

"What the peasants are doing is absolutely right!" Mao exclaimed, delighted. "What they are doing is beautiful."

"Beautiful is the essence of the theory of peasantry and all other revolutionaries. It must be supported by every revolutionary comrade lest he slide into the counterrevolutionary position."

In the spring of 1963, in the article *Where Do Correct Ideas Come from?*, the already victorious revolutionary leader claimed that the ideas of the title did not come from heaven; they are born independently in human imagination. "They come with social experience, and experience alone. They come from three types of experience: struggle for productivity, class struggle, and scientific experiment."

Note that he is talking about continuing struggle. Communists wage this struggle continuously, dooming people to torment and suffering. This is the reason, Comrade Mao concludes, why the comrades should be guided toward the right thinking, the overcoming of obstacles, the minimizing of errors, the rendering of aid to the oppressed masses of the world in accomplishing their great internationalist duty. This is a very revealing thought: helping foreign proletarians in recreating dictatorships with the assistance of loyal Leninist internationalists. That is the kind of assistance he was talking about!

Czech President Vaclav Havel described the effect of totalitarianism, based on personal experience: "Totalitarianism is something a person must experience for himself. From the distance, it is invisible. In our system, violence is spiritual rather than physical. In other words, it is hidden, secret. To outsiders, life here may seem quite normal. You can see people walking in the street, chatting, shopping: to a casual glance, everything seems normal, with no signs of mass murders. A tourist or a foreigner will never see the cruelty of our system."

However, the inhabitants of the land, Havel continues, are eternally dependent "on the magnificence of omnipotent bureaucracy. For every trifle, they have to address an official. They witness a gradual destruction of human spirit, of basic human dignity. People lead lives of constant humiliation. These are the features of the totalitarian system that cannot be filmed by a TV camera nor simply explained to foreign visitors. To see them, one must experience them."

If only Vaclav Havel knew the pleasure we, the Soviet tourists, felt when we traveled in Prague and other Czech cities. We thought we were in a different world, a paradise, because we came from a country where everything was forbidden and in short supply.

Soviet totalitarianism showed in every aspect of life. The system imposed its rules, convictions, worldview, since you were a baby. At 7 or 8 years of age, there was a celebrated ritual of joining the Little October Kids; at 10, it was Young Pioneers; at 14, Komsomol, or Party Youth; at 25 or 30, the Party itself.

Every time, the children had to fill out questionnaires, which included boxes for nationality and information about relatives who had been purged or lived abroad (if they were that lucky). Every time, the parents tried to save their children from the persecution caused by the disagreement between actual information and what was expected. God forbid if they fudged the facts in one of the boxes. The child would become a pariah, unable to join the Little October Kids or any other outfit. Like a leper, he could not enroll in a kind of school or do the kind of studies that he wanted to do. He was condemned, he was never elected on any boards or picked for any conferences, and denied participation at scientific symposiums. The KGB screened everything. And if you were barred from going to Hungary or Yugoslavia on a tourist trip, it meant that a relative had done time or said something wrong. And you never argued because you knew in advance you deserved to be punished before you did it, or perhaps even before you were born, because to be born with this kind of biography was a crime, too.

Since your schooldays you knew what democratic centralism was, why the Party needed membership dues, who was revisionist, who was opportunist, how many times Stalin had escaped from exile and on what dates, who had hidden Lenin outside St. Petersburg and on what armored truck he had entered Petrograd,

Ageless Crimes:
Victims of Totalitarianism Disinterred in Kuropaty.

Leader's Madness. V. Lenin.

The Finale: Lenin Monument Being Dismantled in Riga.
Photo Reuters/Corbis-Bettmann

To Scrap Heap of History:
Kirov Monument Being Dismantled in Baku.

The Ruins of the Empire. *Photo Reuters/Corbis-Bettmann*

Mussolini's Execution. Photo Reuters/Corbis-Bettmann

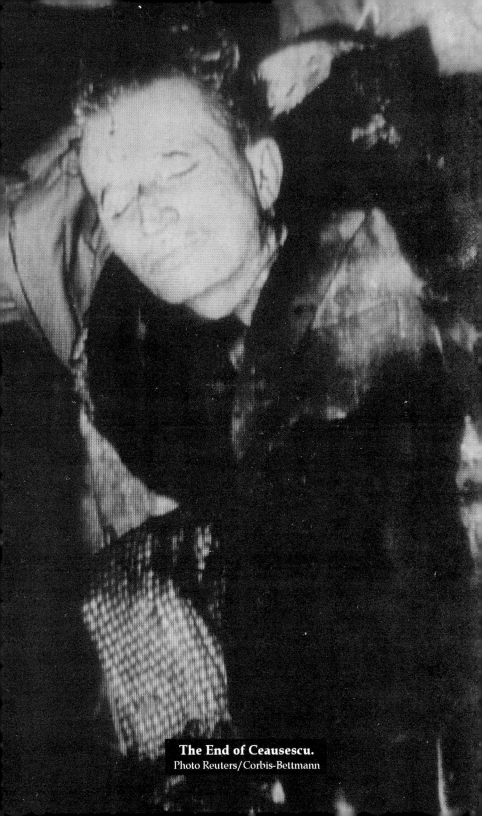

The End of Ceausescu.
Photo Reuters/Corbis-Bettmann

Former Bulgarian Communist Leader Todor Zhivkov under House Arrest. Photo Reuters/Corbis-Bettmann

and when and to whom he cried out, *Yes – there is such a Party!*

Before you were allowed to visit a foreign country – even a Socialist one – you were tormented by various Screening Committees: at your school, at your Party Committee, and other places. You had to know who the General Party Secretary of Rumania, Guatemala, or Ecuador was; why American writer Howard Fast sold out the working people; what Angela Davis said at her trial; what Dimitrov said to Goebbels and how Goebbels responded; and a variety of other absolutely unnecessary facts, ignorance of which would lead to humiliation and denial of an exit visa. And sometimes your "political illiteracy" was discussed at the Party Bureau, at the Committee, at a meeting. Your friends were forced to say things against you they did not believe in. And the lies went on, following you wherever you went. And you did not believe others; but most terribly, you no longer believed yourself.

Not only did the Soviet closed society meet all the requirements of the Popper model; it left his model far behind. In the works of idealist philosophers of the past, the closed totalitarian society presumed that all the efforts will be focused on a single task: the strengthening of the state through the efforts of individual citizens. In the USSR, this concentration on the idea of building a hypothetical Communist society was complemented by the closedness of the society in the literal meaning of the word. The society was deprived of objective information on both domestic and foreign events. All spheres of life were politicized and ideologized: industry, science, culture. If a fitter failed to produce a set quota of screws or nuts, it was a state crime: slowing down the country's advancement to Communism. If a writer or a director put in wrong accents or showed sympathy to a wrong character, he attacked the foundation of Socialism. If a scientist championed Heisenberg's uncertainty principle or Pauling's resonance structures theory, he was assaulting the theoretical foundation of Marxism.

Lenin and Stalin, the main ideologists of the Soviet closed society, created their baby in a planned deliberate fashion. The society was not born spontaneously; its construction followed a precise blueprint that put Machiavelli to shame. If the latter had recommended that the dictator who had obtained power illegitimately should display cruelty only once, the Soviet tyrants kept the country in a state of permanent stress: neither a worker at his lathe nor an executive in his high office had a chance to catch his breath. Purges, arrests, exiles, executions, conspiracies exposed, spies caught, counterrevolutionaries uncovered: even the most prosperous Party official did not know where he would be at the end of the day. Many kept a small kit ready: a toothbrush, a bar of soap, a razor – just in case. The arrests were done at night, and the nightly sound of the boots outside was the horror for many Soviet families.

Were the Founding Fathers sadistic fanatics? Undoubtedly. But the persecution was programmed and steeped in theory. They were building a rational state that would be easy to govern, with the consequences easy to predict. Lenin said, *We do not know and we cannot know the consequences of the revolution.* But they did want to know, to predict, to guide.

Stalin was rumored to be a great psychologist: he knew to charm Feuchtwanger, Roosevelt, or Churchill; he could amaze his guests with his personal modesty; he could pose competent questions to airplane designers and generals. He was rumored to be kind and generous. All through the war he had been promising his President, elderly Kalinin, that he would release his wife from the Gulag. And he did – shortly before Kalinin's death. And he accompanied her at Kalinin's funeral.

As for Bukharin, his friend and the author of the Constitution, who was made into a pariah: without a single word, with one gesture Stalin invited Bukharin to join him atop the Mausoleum. And four months later had him executed.

They say Stalin replaced the Party dictatorship by a personal one. I don't think he veered from Lenin's concept of the Party dictatorship. He merely enriched it by endowing the Party with the privileges that no Secret Service in human history could dream of. The style of Stalin's Politburo was duplicated in every Party branch. Every local Party leader, be it in a city, a town, a village, was a clone of the Great Leader, often wearing the same mufti and the same soft kid-leather boots. A local Party Secretary was in a position to come up with any kind of decision: on enhancing productivity, on violating morality in personal life, on opening a court case. A person dismissed from the Party knew that a police investigation would follow. As a person, you were finished. A tragedy was imminent.

Stalin ordered murders of his relatives, his friends' relatives, his foes' friends – and did it all like a true deranged sadist. As Yuri Karyakin put it, Stalin was an abstract humanist and a practical murderer, an executioner who outdid Robespierre. The latter is reported to say in a rare revelation: "Yes, I am a bloody Messiah! Yes, I build a Golgotha – to others, not to myself! He saved people with His blood, and I'm doing with their own. He forced them to sin, and I'm taking the sin upon myself. He experienced the sweetness of suffering, while I'm suffering an executioner's torment. Who has sacrificed more – he or I?"

Having won the war through enormous sacrifice, Stalin said this on the occasion of the victory: "Our Government has committed many errors. In 1941–42, we had our desperate moments. Another people could say to their government: You have not lived up to our expectations, go away, we'll install another one. But the Russian people did not do that. The Russian people believed that their Government was doing the right thing, and they committed enormous sacrifice to beat Germany."

Some people say that these words reflect Stalin's respect for the people who won the war. To me, it is a satanic joke. It is well known that right after the victory Stalin sent many victors to the Gulag for having been prisoners of war.

Stalin demonstrated his loyalty to Party totalitarianism back in 1929, when he was responding to the congratulations on his fiftieth birthday: "Your greetings and congratulations should be addressed to the great Party of the working class who gave me life and reared me in its image and soul. Have no doubt, Comrades: all my energy, all my abilities, all my blood, drop by drop, are at the disposal of the cause of the working class, the cause of the proletarian revolution and international Communism."

These words are almost completely true, with the exception of the pronoun *"my"*. In reality, Stalin sacrificed to these causes the energy, the abilities, the blood, and the lives of millions of others.

2. SOVIET TOTALITARIANISM = PARTY MEGALITARISM

All totalitarian regimes that existed prior to the Soviet Union were to a various degree justified by historical or economic conditions or the level of public conscience. Philosophers and theorists who helped form public opinion, who foresaw the coming shakeups or interpreted the changes that had already taken place, sincerely believed – at least the best of them did – in the necessity of what they were advocating. As man evolved as a social product, the need to improve state rule, democratize the society as a whole and its separate elements, grew and was put into practice.

Then came the plague of the 20th century: the October Revolution of 1917. Revolutionary fanatics, vengeful terrorists in their ideology and worldview, seduced the masses with their talk of justice, communal good and brotherhood, and popular government. This is how, in defiance of common sense, the Union of the Soviet Socialist Republics came about: a product of a gang of misanthropes skillfully covering their intentions with words about universal brotherhood. *Proletarians of the*

World, Unite! was emblazoned on their banners and printed under the names of all their newspapers. The country both emerged and existed as a result of a non-stop struggle. They did not just "work"; they always "struggled to achieve labor feats." Not just "learn"; always "struggled through the barriers of knowledge." Not just "resolve" their numerous problems; they "extended a helping hand to the fraternal peoples of all continents."

The country was created and governed by criminals; not even political prisoners but plain gangsters. Both their methods and execution were typical of the underworld. It was the first time in the history of mankind that a bunch of semiliterate self-imposed recidivists ruled one-sixth of the world and kept the rest of the world on edge for three-quarters of a century. As is the norm in gangland, they kept killing one another, making space for the top capo, Stalin. But there were many others, as hateful and murderous.

What court would pronounce judgment on the leaders and executioners of that system? What curses should be addressed to those who are gone and to those who still remain?

I will cite a few items from the list of crimes that writer Vladimir Soloukhin has charged the Soviet Communist Party and totalitarian regime with.

On October 25, 1917, a group of revolutionary extremists acting in the Party's name arrested the Provisional Government and dismissed the Parliament; that is, it used violent means to usurp power in Russia, which by then was already a republic.

This group seized power not only by violence but through deception as well; not for the benefit of prosperity of the country's population, but in order to conduct a social and political experiment and use the country's population and natural resources as materials for that experiment.

As soon as the group realized that 90 percent of the population are unwilling to participate in this utopian experiment, instead of aborting the experiment and conceding power, they unleashed a reign of terror which eventually took the lives of over one-third of population.

In the name of the Party was unleashed a bloody fraternal war; the best minds of the nation who survived the war had to emigrate.

In order to satisfy its political ambitions, the Party sanctioned the murder of the Czar's family, including innocent children and women.

Throughout their rule, the rulers expropriated bread from the farmers and thus repeatedly caused famine that took millions of lives and resulted in cannibalism, including that of children.

Numerous revolts caused by terror were suppressed with yet more terror. Uprisings in Putilovsky Plant, Kolpino, Izhorsk, Kronstadt, Yaroslavl, Astrakhan, Izhevsk, Perm, Penza, Tambov, and other places throughout Siberia and Central Asia, were drowned in blood.

In the name of the Party, following a decree signed by Yakov Sverdlov, Special Troops (ChON) committed mass murders of Don and Kuban Cossacks, including the destruction of whole villages with women and children.

Under the pretext of fighting famine (caused by the rulers) the Party burglarized and expropriated the riches collected through centuries in churches and monasteries.

Hundreds of mosques and Koran schools were destroyed, and mullahs executed.

In 1936 in Buryatiya alone, 36 lamaseries were destroyed, along with Tibetan libraries and other historic, artistic, and material values.

Across the country, 90 percent of monasteries and cathedrals were destroyed; 450 in Moscow alone, including Russia's holiest one, the Cathedral of Christ the Savior.

In 1929–30, the Party conducted forced collectivization of farmers, in which six million farms were destroyed. In Kazakhstan, millions of cattle were destroyed.

The above collectivization resulted in the peasants' alienation from the land and motivated labor. It led to what we now call the de-farming of Russia. Agriculture decayed, villages emptied, land is overrun by weed.

Instead of pursuing the prosperity of the State and people, the Party was pursuing a utopian world revolution and world communist system and used an enslaved, raped country as a resource for the implementation of this idea. For decades, the Party had been robbing this rich country. The forests were cut down in haste, and the timber was floated down all northbound rivers, which led to the spoilage of both the timber and the rivers, whose bottoms are waterlogged with thirty layers of sunk timber. Oil, gas, gold, gemstones, rare metals, and silver were sold in raw form. Furs and fish were sold, with the proceeds channeled to the party's needs, away from the public. Gigantic dams and reservoirs were built at maniacal pace, and millions of hectares of fertile land were flooded. Erosion of unique Voronezh soils, poisoning of the Baikal Lake, complete spoilage of the Aral Sea, and up to 30 millions of hectares of cattle-grazing steppe in Kazakhstan, Hakassia, and Altai fell victim to the virgin land reclamation.

For decades, the country was covered with a chain of camps that ground to dust millions of human lives.

The system based on violence, oppression, and lawlessness destroyed society, its morality and humanity, and led to total alcoholism and blossoming of crime.

Paralyzed with fear, one-fifth of the population were recruited as secret informers and thus were morally raped and despoiled, for an informer cannot be considered a morally complete person (the "one-fifth" statistic was revealed by Khruschev when he was denouncing Beria's deeds).

The Party began lying on the first day of its rule and has never stopped lying. Thus, having made the lies into the law of the land, it indoctrinated the population in lies and corrupted it beyond measure. The Party needed the lies: the dictatorship of radical revolutionaries was passed along as the dictatorship of the proletariat; this group of half-baked intellectuals pronounced itself as the vanguard of the working class and peasantry. Another lie was passing the rape of the land as concern for people's welfare; unparalleled enslavement as unparalleled freedom; impoverishment of the population as prosperity; in short, the black was passed off as the white.

For decades, the ruling group, acting in the name of the Party, has been forcing its will on the population, suffering no disobedience or dissidence and thus corrupting people's psychology by turning them into obedient, silent slaves (the disobedient and vocal ones were systematically destroyed).

In the name of the Party, entire nations – Volga Germans, Chechens, Ingushes, Karachayevs, Crimean Tatars, Balkars, Georgian Turks – were ejected from their historic lands into Kazakh steppes, deserts, and taiga forests, where three-quarters of them perished.

Finally, as a result of its actions the Party (which has always led the nation forth) has

taken the country to the limit. It plunged
Russia into the abyss of economic, demo-
graphic, social, interethnic, and ecological di-
sasters to the extent that getting back on its
feet is an open question.

I realize that each ethnic group presents this predatory system with its own bill, its own list of crimes
committed against it. This system has destroyed
Azerbaijan's best, most educated people; it attempted
to turn the remaining ones into obedient slaves, to
destroy our roots, our faith, our memory; in order to
impose its own values, it put in power the most corrupt ones.

It is today's tragedy in former Soviet republics that
many Party executives, the leaders of yesteryear, never
repenting, quickly donned democratic garb and are
passing themselves off as people's saviors, while continuing the same policy of deception and physical and
moral depredation of the people. Yesterday's Communist dictators turned into "Fathers of the Nation," brand-
new idols of democracy. They put their pictures on
bank notes and street corners, along with their quotes;
towns and streets and factories are being named after
them. Suddenly, they have found religion, which only
yesterday they tried to uproot with decrees and directives. They have adopted new democratic-sounding
laws which they are happily ignoring and using as cover
for their true deeds. They have learned English words
– *legitimacy, consensus, business* – and use them to subordinate those still enslaved by yesterday's fears and lies.
But however they polish their true identity, they still
carry the imprint of totalitarianism.

My direct experience of Soviet totalitarianism makes me give preference to Popper's definition. I define Soviet totalitarianism as Party megalitarism, which represents the highest concentration of all power in the hands of the Party and its Leader Maximus or whatever he calls himself. In my opinion, there are certain features that constitute the ABCs of totalitarianism which help identify it regardless of its outer appearance. These features include:

Concentration of power in the hands of one person who decides all the key issues. This regretful practice of making "power-based" decisions by a sole person was established by Lenin at the dawn of Bolshevism. As they took power, the Bolsheviks usurped decision-making; first it was a small group, and then it got reduced to one person. Officially, the decisions were ascribed to the Politburo or the Government, which was a pure formality.

This style did not alter through seven changes of Kremlin rule and has been preserved in most newly formed states.

In December 1927, at the Party's 15th Congress, V. Kuybyshev, the Chairman of the Central Auditing Committee (CAC), announced: "I state in the name of CAC that Comrade Stalin, the Party's General Secretary, is the person who has been able to bring together the Party's best cadre. In the name of CAC I state that this leadership and this General Secretary are what the Party needs in order to proceed to further victories."

After a speech like this, even formal assurance of collective decision-making was no longer required. Stalin knew best what the Party – the people – the country – needed. He successfully compensated his own ignorance of political and economic development by adopting the ideas and suggestions of his comrades, whom he murdered soon thereafter.

This feature was astutely reported by Nikolai Volski, who emigrated from the Soviet Union to France in 1929:

> Stalin adores his mechanical piano player. As he keeps sipping his favorite wine, delivered to him personally from the Caucasus, he keeps pumping the pedals and "plays piano." He forgets that it is a mechanical toy. He seems to be really thinking that it is his fingers that are performing his favorite, the Toreador's March from *Carmen*. One might say that he plays with other people's ideas in social and political life. Unblushingly, he takes ideas, inserts them into his head the way you insert disks into the player piano, and... the piano plays.
>
> In 1924, along with Bukharin, Rykov, and others, he sharply criticized Preobrazhensky, one of the opposition leaders who proposed that "Socialist accumulation" be created by using what they termed then as feudal exploitation of peasants. In 1929, as if nothing had happened, he makes Preobrazhensky's suggestions the keystone of his policy.
>
> In 1924–25, influenced by Bukharin and Rykov, he resisted Trotsky's idea of superindustrialization. By 1929, he shifts to support

this superindustrialization in the most barbaric form. One musical disk has been replaced by another; the music goes on. While adopting another man's idea that he opposed only yesterday and claiming it his own, Stalin generally perceives it in an extended form and on a distorted scale. Struck by the stolen idea, he wants to act on it right away; he has the power, too, and this is how in his hands many ideas turn into an equivalent of a knife in the hands of a madman.

Lenin was aware of Stalin's main qualities, obtuseness and rudeness, yet prized him for his loyalty. While talking to Nogin, he admitted, "Stalin's misfortune is that he is fond of simple truths and does not realize that frequently such truths are actually the most complicated ones. Besides, he has no sense of proportion and tends to overdo things. If he were a cook in the Army, he would be putting too much salt in the soldiers' borscht, and every day the soldiers would be dumping it on his head. On the other hand, I doubt that even this punishment would turn Stalin into a good cook."

This type of a Soviet leader turned out to have nine lives. So many Soviet leaders grabbed others' ideas like madmen with knives, imposing them on the country and hatching out nonsensical projects and plans. Let us recall Khruschev's obsession with corn, Gorbachev's anti-alcohol campaign, and Andropov's raids on potential malingerers caught outside their workplaces.

Even today, "madmen with knives" continue adopting and imposing distorted ideas, while insisting that they care about national welfare. With these decisions and directives, they are robbing not only the population of today but many generations to come, wasting both natural and human resources.

Excessive concentration of both legal and illegal capital in one person's hands. When Soviet leaders were assisting fraternal parties or presenting gifts to visiting VIPs, they were treating the State Treasury as their own pocket. Can you imagine the French President presenting a visitor with a gift from the storage of the Louvre or Pompidou Center? Or the American President summoning the President of Chase Manhattan and asking him to make out a check for establishing a Democratic Party in Sri Lanka or in Russia?

The Soviet leaders were using The Hermitage, The Tretyakov Gallery, and even the Kremlin's Armory as their personal warehouses. Stalin handed currency from the State Bank to representatives of fraternal Communist parties without blinking an eye.

Post-Soviet dictators are not as primitive. Yet they have greater resources at their disposal: foreign credits, hard-currency raw-material contracts, expenditures for defense and the army, commercial contracts for various goods and food supplies, and the humanitarian aid. It does not take a rich imagination to figure out how a totalitarian leader would resolve these issues. Is there a civilized country whose leadership would assume exclusive authority in these areas? What is the purpose of concentrating these powers in the hands of one person or a group of persons?

Here is another shameful tradition going back to the Soviet days. Let us take a Caucasian or a Central

Asian republic. Considering today's productivity levels, the worker efficiency in the manufacturing sector is not very high: let us say, $2,000 per capita a year, or $170 a month. In a country like this, an average monthly salary is between $10 and $40. Of the remaining $130–$160, the State Treasury gets perhaps 30 percent. The rest, to the tune of millions of dollars, vanishes. Its routes are being mapped out and monitored by the same Decision-Maker. As a result, foreign accounts feature amounts comparable to a national budget.

Another aspect in the development of the newly independent states. As a rule, the activity of foreign companies there is limited by the framework of more or less reasonable taxes and duties. At the same time, local manufacturing and commerce are being stifled, both legally and illegally, by excessive taxes, in keeping with the Soviet traditions. Naturally, this drives up the market prices and forces consumers to purchase inferior goods from foreign suppliers; but most important, it stifles the growth of homegrown businesses. What is the reason? Interests of State officialdom? Artificial containment of large-scale homegrown business? State-approved racket? New ways of obtaining illegal capital? Most likely, all of the above.

Appearance of democratic pluralism and liquidation of competition. Soviet leaders have always told the world public that in the Soviet Union, the broadest spectrum of opinion on various political and economic issues existed and was encouraged. In reality, throughout most of the Soviet period, it was a chorus of voices singing paeans to the regime and its creators.

All the political parties that were in coalition with the Bolsheviks during the revolution were literally eliminated. Under the Soviets, the Mensheviks, the Constitutional Democrats, the Socialist Revolutionaries, and the Anarchists were locked up in camps far tougher than the ones they had known under the Czar. The war on their former allies was waged by the entire top leadership of the Bolshevik Party, including Trotsky, Zinovyev, Kamenev, Bukharin, and Rykov. They did not suspect that, once they were done with their dastardly deed, they would fall prey to Stalin in turn. Stalin conducted his terror step by step, and at each stage conspired with those who would fall the next time. However, for justice's sake, we must admit that the terror was not started by Stalin, who was so vividly described by Osip Mandelshtam in a 1933 poem:

> His fat fingers are as oily as worms
> His words are as true as ten-pound weights
> His roach-like moustache is grinning
> His boots are shining
> Around him, the riffraff of pencil-necked leaders
> He toys with the services of semi-humans
> One whistles, one meows, one whines
> He's the only one who can point his finger
> He forges decrees like horseshoes
> One gets it in the groin, another in the brow
> His every execution is a thief's banquet
> Rules by a broad chest of an Osset.

Lenin was the first to start eliminating his political opponents shortly after the Bolshevik Party – the party of terror – was established. Stalin, however, turned the elimination of his former allies into a farce. First

Zinovyev and Kamenev helped Stalin fell Trotsky. Then, aided by Bukharin, Rykov, and Tomsky, Stalin felled Zinovyev and Kamenev. And only then, having concentrated power in his hands, aided by less educated but greedier satraps, did Stalin eliminate Bukharin and Company. Before that, he stole an idea or two from each of them, and then arranged a show trial that involved broad support from peasants and workers who unanimously condemned the "Enemies of the People." Each victim was labeled a foreign agent. For example, Tukhachevsky and other top brass were tried as German agents. Later, Khruschev will continue Stalin's methods by labeling Beria an English and French spy.

Today, it seems like dementia, but a totalitarian regime does not lend itself to healthy reasoning. The machine of state terror and misinformation worked hard, and many naively believed the balderdash. Unfortunately, we see some of it even today.

At each stage, *Pravda* printed the opposition's declarations, which were followed by the condemnation of these turncoats as the revisionists of Lenin's great doctrine – signed by "conscientious" workers. Outwardly, this appeared to be an active debate where each party was given a voice. Yet in fact it was an odious persecution of former allies. It was a fight between spiders in a jar, monitored and guided by the only one who could "point his finger."

Such was Stalin's pluralism, which in various versions is being implemented today by the followers of any "Father of the Nations." It is still the same ominous scenario: in order to get rid of the most ardent opponents, some allies are being brought in; then another group is being brought in to eliminate the second one; and so on, until the power is concentrated in one person warmly supported by the people.

People must be kept in poverty so that, on the one hand, they remain law-abiding; on the other, in order to survive, they have to resort to crime. The Bolsheviks and their successors have always been attracted to the idea of ruling a hungry, impoverished people. Its attraction lies in the fact that a hungry man will always have to steal, and therefore there will always be evidence against him. The Soviet regime provided people with broad opportunities to steal state property that in reality belonged to no one. In exchange, the regime gained the right to punish practically anyone at any given time: there was always a pretext. People were punished for stolen stalks of wheat, a packet of candy, or a piece of sausage.

The Party General Secretary Leonid Brezhnev once revealed that a Soviet man's salary can hardly be called such: in his student years he, too, had to resort to theft in order to survive.

Shortly before his death, Nikolai Bukharin, who participated in developing the policy of wide-scale punishment, stated proudly: "Our iron-clad discipline, our monolith cohesion, the unanimity of our wills – these are and will always be the inherent characteristics of the Party. Among us Bolsheviks this is recognized as an axiom – a truth that requires no proof."

He was right. The Bolsheviks unanimously sentenced him to death. Prior to that, allied with Stalin, he defended the Party unity, criticized the opposition, and attacked Krupskaya, but even then he was already doomed.

Perhaps he was doomed even earlier, when Stalin swore over Lenin's coffin: "We Communists are special people. We are made of a special substance. We are the ones who make up the army of the great proletarian strategist – the great Lenin's army. There is no higher honor than being a soldier in this army. No higher honor than being a member of the party founded and led by Comrade Lenin. Not everyone deserves to be a member. Not everyone can weather the storms and ordeals that this membership entails. The sons of the working class, the sons of need and struggle, the sons of fantastic ordeals and heroic efforts – they are the ones who, first and foremost, should be the members of our party."

Bukharin was no son "of need and... fantastic ordeals," but he was heedless of these words then; he thought it was a boilerplate funeral speech. But in fact it was an appeal to eliminate the opposition, for each one of them bore the mark of Judas. Stalin knew what he was doing: he provided an opportunity to sin, but the sinner would not evade punishment.

This quality of Stalin's is typical of all dictators, including post-Soviet ones. The state is maintained in such a condition that no one should ever expect mercy. And the sinner is condemned by those closest to him, for they themselves have sinned. And everyone gets his turn. Yet for some reason no one draws conclusions. Why? The dictator's strategy is so primitive.

116

Any sign of opposing the dictator is termed as an attempt of coup d'état. Staging of conspiracies and attempted assassinations. This is the dictators' favorite show, in which the masses partake with joyous enthusiasm. All you need to do is to call on them, day or night. You can ask for their help; you will promote the loudest mouths, which will be later eliminated under any pretext. But the most important thing is to take advantage of an assassination attempt, be it real or faked. It is simpler to stage an attempt and eliminate a favorite ally, and then tighten the nuts – no one will oppose that.

An assassination attempt, whether staged or real, is an excellent pretext to take revenge on strong rivals and, more important, to draw popular attention. Thus people will be distracted from their genuine problems. When you're in the crowd, you're not tormented by hunger and thirst as much.

People can be told repeatedly that an assassination was being plotted against the head of the state, and all his foes (as a rule, members of the opposition) have committed high treason.

In Stalin's day, tens of thousands people arrested by secret police "confessed" they had plotted an assassination of Stalin. But the dictator wanted more, and so their testimony was used for developing entire scenarios of terrorist acts having been plotted, involving hundreds of thousands of people, whose guilt was proved as "evident." Similar trials still take place under totalitarian regimes, though in a more sophisticated fashion. Attempted assassinations of the head of state are uncovered in practically every country. According to statistics, American law enforcement receives about 2,000 reports a year about attempts on the President's life, most of which are imaginary. In Russia, this amount comes to 500. But in none of these other countries are people ever told about these "attempts," no mass debate is held, and no one exhorts people to tighten their ranks against the enemy. Such methods are necessary attributes of totalitarian regimes, designed to distract starving, impoverished people from their problems, and they will be used as long as these regimes exist.

In the United States, a rare President is not immune to this threat. Four times in history, terrorists were effective: Lincoln, Garfield, McKinley, and Kennedy were all murdered. But in none of these cases was the assassination regarded as an attempted coup d'état. Naturally, the President is the head of state but not *the* state. Killing the President will not accomplish a coup d'état in a country with a genuine sense of state and, consequently, stability.

However, it is possible under totalitarian regimes that lack stability, where the state does not exist for the people's benefit, and is perceived as the rule of one person. In this situation, any general or even a major can eliminate the dictator and proclaim himself the new one.

If an attempt on the head of state is interpreted as an attempted coup d'état, it means that the state institutions are not functioning, that there is no stability no genuine sense of statehood, and the country is under a totalitarian regime.

The seeming stability that follows a string of repressions resembles a house of cards removable at a single blow. This is what I referred to in my interview with the *New Times* magazine, when I said that "stability in Azerbaijan cannot be propped by force." I'm not talking about Azerbaijan alone: all totalitarian regimes are infected with this disease.

Falsification of history, of economic laws, of current information – total falsification across the board. As every new Soviet leader came to power, the history of key events had to be rewritten. Certain Civil War battles or Second World War campaigns had to be assigned higher importance at the expense of others. In the former case, the person most responsible for victory was originally Trotsky, then Stalin, then Frunze, then Budyonny, then Voroshilov. Similarly, the crucial part in World War II was played by Stalin, then Zhukov, then Khruschev – Brezhnev – Zhukov again. Similarly, certain themes were promoted heavily: today the spotlight was on corn growing, tomorrow on the chemical industry, then on anti-alcohol propaganda – all depending on the current ruler's hobbyhorse. History was turned into a masked ball, with masks falling as soon as the dictator was removed.

Now, too, similar comedies are being played out in newly independent states. Books are being written and lavishly published; the leaders' biographies are being compiled, starting at their embryonic stage. Amazing facts are being trotted forth in order to impress a common reader: for example, the story of Kim Il Sung meeting a tiger.

Once, the story goes, the young Kim Il Sung was fishing on a riverbank, pondering his people's destiny.

119

Suddenly, an Ussurian tiger emerged from the bush – perhaps he had traveled all the way from Siberia. The future leader and teacher of the Korean people stared the predator down, and it retired back into the bush with its tail between its legs.

It is a useful fact for other dictators' biographies. Kim's sage look is the look of a great seer and peace-maker, a look of a teacher capable of solving life's most dangerous and complicated problems.

There are similar myths galore in the history of to-talitarian states. While the leader is alive and orating, the mass media fill the airtime with stories of nonexist-ent achievements reached in negotiation with other heads of state. He is called "great"; then, "one of the greatest"; finally, "the greatest." He begins to believe his own lies and fills up with awareness of his impor-tance and infallibility.

There are other typical characteristics of totalitar-ian regimes, regardless of their geographic and historic location:

- Hanging on to power at all costs.
- Suppressing democracy to the end.
- Installing a pyramidal power structure at all levels of authority; selecting loyal flunkeys; regularly over-hauling all power structures.
- Forcing a state of animal fear on the citizenry.
- Installing a widespread system of secret informers.
- Within the chain of authority, creating "forbidden areas" for common citizens for various reasons other than the dictator's clan system.
- Repression – repression – repression.

Undoubtedly, a totalitarian regime is less sophisticated than a democratic one. The dictator does not need to be an intellectual; however, he must be cruel – or, rather, exceptionally cruel and treacherous. As a rule, his average intellect goes with an unbalanced psychological profile. However, psychotic abnormalities are no obstacle.

The Soviet Union was long ruled by unbalanced people. Lenin issued his last directives in a state of complete dementia. Stalin, according to many doctors, including a renowned scientist like Bekhterev, suffered from paranoia and other pathological manias. Brezhnev and Chernenko were practically insane in their last months on the throne.

A remarkable example from American history: President Washington was faced with a dilemma. One, he would make concessions to the military and leave them with full control of the army. For this, he would need to dismiss the insubordinate Congress and replace it with an obedient one. Two, he could make concessions to the Congress that demanded army reform and the curtailment of Presidential powers.

Washington chose the latter, as more fitting to American democratic principles and ideals. It was not an easy decision, but that's where a democratic state is different from a totalitarian one: to promote democracy, a true democrat would consent to the weakening of his own powers, including retirement. Nixon is a good example.

Democracy is not comfortable for leaders: it forces them to follow the Constitution, democratic principles, and public interest. But this is the only worthy and true way of the nation.

Winston Churchill remarked, with truly British humor: "Democracy is the worst form of government, but mankind has not come up with anything better yet." He also penned a few scathing and correct observations on the nature of dictators:

"Dictators ride to and fro upon tigers from which they dare not dismount. And the tigers are getting hungry."

"One of the disadvantages of dictatorships is that the dictator is often dictated to by others, and what he did to others may often be done back again to him."

"You see these dictators on their pedestals surrounded by the bayonets of their soldiers and truncheons of their police…. They boast and vaunt themselves before the world, yet in their hearts there is unspoken fear. They are afraid of words and thoughts stirring at home – all the more powerful because forbidden. The tiniest mouse of thought appears in the room, and the mightiest potentates are thrown into panic."

According to Churchill, a dictatorship is "the monstrous child of emergency," "the fetish worship of one man."

Naturally, every totalitarian regime has a creator: a dictator who either inherited his position or usurped it. One has to note that the dictator type largely determines the type of dictatorship. On the basis of historical empirical analysis, dictators can be divided into three groups:

Ideological dictators. This type has a firm plan of action that he considers obligatory and natural for all other nations. He sincerely believes that this plan meets people's heartfelt needs and pursues the noblest ends. For this type, installing a totalitarian regime is not an end in itself, but rather a means to an end.

Power dictators. Their main objective is holding on to power by all means, and a totalitarian regime is a perfect tool. Their objectives do not reach beyond those of tribal leaders; they just want to remain on the throne as long as possible. Such regimes exist on the American continent, in Arab countries, and in Asia, where so-called Presidents get reelected with enviable constancy for the last thirty or forty years, and always in a landslide.

Narcissistic dictators. These dictators are self-content, enamored with themselves, believe in their infallibility, exceptionality, and superbrilliance. They assume power for long periods of time, to make sure their families, both nuclear and extended, get enriched, and they have something was left for their satraps. They assume power in order to become part of the history.

The two latter types can rule also in authoritarian regimes.

After the October coup, it took Lenin and Stalin eight years (to 1925) to eliminate existing parties of Mensheviks, Social Revolutionaries, etc., and then another eleven years (to 1936) to eliminate all "dissidents," or potential rivals within their own party.

How long will it take new dictators to eliminate their opposition and stamp out dissidence?

How many hellish nightmares do people still have to go through?

3. Inevitability of Collapse of Totalitarian Regimes and Its Consequences

Shortly after the revolution, Nikolai Bukharin – the Party's pet, Lenin called him – carefully developed a plan of eliminating the social groups that in his mind posed obstacles in building Socialism. These groups included former landowners, industrialists, retailers, bankers, stockbrokers; aristocrats in administrative jobs; factory managers; civil servants, churchmen, military officers, intellectuals, academics, scientists, well-to-do farmers, and the whole middle class in general.

The program was approved by Lenin and in many ways scrupulously implemented. Most importantly, there were many volunteers to help the Party rid the society of its elite. The author of this bloody program was less fortunate: Stalin's court charged him with membership in a Trotskyist counterrevolutionary organization. Taking into account Bukharin's fundamental confession, Procurator General Vyshinsky sentenced him to death.

Shortly before death, Bukharin wrote:

> I'm leaving this life. But I'm not lowering my head for the proletarian axe, which has to be both ruthless and virtuous. I feel my helplessness in the face of the colossal hellish machine that, perhaps employing medieval methods, is fabricating organized slander and acting with bold confidence. At present the NKVD [Secret Police] is an or-

ganization of idea-less, corrupt, well-paid
bureaucrats who, using the high authority
of their predecessor Cheka and pleasing
Stalin's pathological suspiciousness – I fear
to say more – are doing their dastardly deeds
in search of medals and glory.

Bukharin's destiny was shared by Lenin's entire Old
Guard, including their relatives, close and removed;
by witnesses and participants of revolutionary and
prerevolutionary activities; as well as by millions of
others capable of saying or recalling something.

The fortunate one was Malenkov, a participant and
initiator of many bloody purges. It turned out that, after leaving his high-ranking position, he became a
member of a church choir, began observing Orthodox
church rites, atoned for his sins, and asked to be given
a church burial. I believe that his example was followed
by many other criminals of the regime, who became
zealous Christians and Moslems. Will they all be for-
given by God?

In other words, once the creators of the despotic
regime fell prey to their own invention, they arrived at
the conclusion about its inhumanity and uselessness. Is
this not the most telling sign of doom for the system
based on sin, lies, and hatred of humanity?

Did not the Evil Empire implacably and inevitably
approach its death from its very first day? Was not its
development a gradual slide into the abyss?

Zbigniew Brzezinski, who analyzed brilliantly the
reasons for the death of Soviet Communism in his book
The Grand Failure, concludes:

The phenomenon of Communism is an historical tragedy. Generated by impatient idealism that rejected the injustice of status quo, it strove towards a better, more humane society, yet it led to mass oppression. It optimistically reflected faith in the power of reason, capable of creating a perfect society. In the name of morally motivated social engineering, it mobilized the most powerful human sentiments: love of mankind and hatred for oppression. Thus it succeeded in drawing in the brightest minds and the most idealistic souls, yet it led to most horrifying crimes of our – and not only our – century.

Moreover, Communism represented a misguided effort to impose total rationality on social phenomena. It proceeded from the assumption that a literate, politically aware society can control social evolution and guide socioeconomic transformations towards designated goals.

While recognizing Brzezinski's fine analytic intellect, I will take exception to his conclusions. In my opinion, similar errors are in general typical of other Western intellectuals who tried to find the minutest shreds of reason in the Communist plague that spread across the planet in the first quarter of the 20th century.

No: the phenomenon of Communism is not a historical tragedy, but the most vicious crime against humanity.

No: the brand of Communism that took over in Russia did not contain the slightest desire to do away with existing injustices. From the very start the Bolsheviks deliberately wrought yet greater injustices as they planned mass murder of people who did not fit in with their doctrine.

No: Marx, Lenin, Stalin, and their followers had no desire to strive for a better, more humane society. The construction of the mass concentration camp, the barracks with forced labor, was planned and implemented from the very start. Mass crimes of the Communist regime are not the result of revolutionary mass movements; they are an original impulse of the system.

No: there was no morally motivated social engineering, no belief in reason, no love of mankind and hatred for oppression. From the start, it practiced a different attitude toward the people on whom the experiment was being performed. The vicious fanatics of the bloody revolution hated the same people whom they summoned under their banners; they lied to the people while seducing them with slogans like *Peace to shacks, war to palaces! We Want Peace – Bread – Land!*

No: there was no morality, for from the very start, quite consciously, the Bolsheviks appealed to the basest human emotions – envy, greed, spite. From day one, they set out to create an empire of informers, of little children betraying their parents for the sake of Honor Certificates and other handouts.

No: the regime's deeds, decisions, and directives contained not an iota of rationality. To the contrary, it was an irrational pile, moved solely by public inertia.

127

No: from day one, there was not the slightest respect for mind and intellect. Moreover, it was Lenin who remarked famously that the intelligentsia is not the brains of the people, but rather its shit. It was he who initiated banishment and elimination of the best minds of Russia and her colonies.

Thus, in my opinion, Soviet Communism represented an antihuman, unnatural growth, doomed as an embryo to failure and contempt of history. It was an evil experiment on humanity, aimed against natural human aspirations and desires.

Nevertheless, Mr. Brzezinski quite correctly describes the phases of the Soviet state's approach to its end: "(1) Under Lenin: a totalitarian Party aimed at total social reconstruction; (2) under Stalin: a totalitarian State with a totally subordinate society; (3) under Brezhnev: a totally rotting State governed by the corrupt totalitarian Party."

I would also add here the last Andropov-Gorbachev phase: the death throes of the regime. While the leaders were relatively low-key, this phase is tainted by the blood of the events in Vilnius, Tbilisi, and Baku, where the departing regime was leaving the bodies of the innocent in its wake. It knew no other way of leaving...

The consequences of Phase 4 are still with us: the fighting goes on in Central Asia, in Chechnya, in Northern Caucasus, and in Trans-Caucasus.

The deceased regime seems to be "reaching" for the democratic changes from the netherworld. The pro-democracy rallies are over, the Popular Fronts have fallen apart, and almost everywhere the former Party bosses returned to their offices, now acting as top Democrats. Without even an apology – no one is talking about atonement – they settled down, looked around, and slid into their new role, one of spiritual leaders. A farce of sorts, and a tragicomedy of collapse.

One may have a feeling that the former KGB Colonel Lyubimov was right when he posited in his fantastic thriller that *perestroika* was designed by the KGB who wanted to shake up and invigorate the country. So it was another Satanic presentation? Or rather a punishment for people's failure of nerve, for their fear that they never managed to get out of their systems? Can it be true that this powerful stirring, this ardor, could not last beyond a few authorized rallies and demonstrations? Can it be that people never learned to "squeeze a slave out of themselves?"

I suspect the reasons are much simpler. Experienced politicos who had cut their teeth while plotting in the Party's backrooms now took advantage of the situation; they manipulated democracy groups against one another, pulled on new masks, and once again fooled the people – could it be true?

They had something to lose. They were just about to face the trial of the Party for its iniquities; each of them was on the verge of being handcuffed. And now they got off scot-free, climbed back onto their thrones, and got back to robbing the people – but no longer in useless rubles. Now it was dollars and other hard currency. Why not? How are they inferior to other monarchs and dictators? How about Fidel, who saved for a rainy day a nest egg comparable to Cuba's national budget? Or Saddam Hussein, who beat the civilized world in financial terms? His phrase about having won the war against Kuwait may seem misspoken. But he knows what he is talking about; in that war he made out like a bandit – which means he won.

Ditto for these former dictators now wearing democratic clothes. They never lost a battle. The losers were the mothers, the wives, the children, who lost their relatives and hope in the future. The dictators won big in all war theaters in the former Evil Empire.

Finally, a few words about the lot of dictators.

Today, the Lenin monument with a noose around his neck is used in the ad campaign for the RCN phone company, which maintains that no empire lasts forever. The leaders' gypsum and bronze heads are covered with moss and eaten by mutant worms. The frighteningly stupid mugs of all seven Soviet dictators are painted on matryoshka dolls.

I wonder if the dictators of the new independent states are pondering this lot.

I wonder if they feel a little pinch in their hearts as they suspect that their tombstones will be overrun by weeds, and their likenesses will be cast out to the same heaps where now rests the bronze Felix Dzerjinsky, the founder of the KGB.

I wonder if they are afraid of the 21st century – the century when mankind's blinders will fall off, the century of informational progress.

I wonder if they think of the bitter example of Mobutu and Pol Pot, rejected and redundant.

Or, perhaps, some of them are hoping to be exceptions to the rule.

Chapter Three

OPEN SOCIETY AND DEMOCRACY

1. FROM PERICLES TO MODERNITY

Let me once again refer you to some ideas formulated by Karl Popper in his *Open Society and Its Enemies.*

As remarked earlier, the champions of totalitarian systems – here Plato and Marx agree, despite a gap in time and space – justify any social norms and criteria by their usefulness and fitness for the solid state mechanism. According to Plato, even "genuine happiness" can be achieved only through genuine justice, which is defined as precise correlation between a citizen and his social function – a ruler finds happiness in ruling, a soldier in fighting, a slave in slavery – since the objective of the totalitarian system is universal happiness, as opposed to the happiness of individual members or a specific social group.

Pericles, Democritus, Herodotus, and other great Greeks claimed that man-made institutions of law, tradition, language, limitations, and others are creations of human reason, rather than principles provided by nature. Therefore, only man is responsible for them. Later, their followers developed ideas of antislavery, rational protectionism, antinationalism – in other words, the principles of the world community of man. Above all of them rises Socrates, who criticized democratic Athens in the name of the purity of the democratic idea.

Popper describes the ideas of another Greek philosopher, Democritus, on the makeup and the principles of an open democratic society: "We should refrain from committing wrong deeds not from fear but from perception of truth....Virtue is based primarily on respect for others.... Every man is a miniature world.... A poor democracy is better than a prosperous aristocracy or monarchy, just as freedom is better than slavery."

Pericles, whose rule is considered the Golden Age of Athenian democracy, said about the open society: "Our political system does not compete with institutions which are elsewhere in force. We do not copy our neighbors, but try to be an example. Our administration favors the man instead of the few: this is why it is called a democracy....The freedom we enjoy extends also to ordinary life; we are not suspicious of one another, and do not nag our neighbor if he chooses to go his own way....But this freedom does not make us lawless. We are taught to respect the magistrates and the laws, and never to forget that we must protect the injured. We are also taught to observe unwritten laws whose sanction lies only in the universal feeling of what is right.....Although only a few may originate a policy, we are all able to judge it....We believe that happiness is a fruit of freedom."

To Popper, these words contain the true spirit of the generation of great Greek thinkers, as well as a political program of an individualist and democrat who understands well that democracy cannot be affirmed by a simple slogan like *People must rule*, democracy is possible only if humanist principles and belief in reason are observed.

Faith in humanity, in human reason, in equal justice for all, constitutes the principal distinction of the open society. Socrates continued to criticize democratic society from the position of a democrat and paid for his principles with his life. These principles of public behavior largely determine the foundation of modern civilized states: dominating role of intellect and reason as the universal medium of communication, intellectual honesty and self-criticism, the idea of justice, and finally the presumption that it is better to be a victim of injustice than impose injustice on others.

I would like to quote Popper regarding the historical lesson of closed ancient societies. These words are especially vital when applied to the birth and death of the Soviet Union – one of the most despotic totalitarian empires in history.

> Stalling political change cannot serve as a means and will not bring happiness. We can never go back to the closed society's unsupported purity and beauty. Our dream of paradise cannot be realized on Earth. Once we begin relying on reason and use our ability for critical analysis, once we realize the call for personal responsibility and thus responsibility for encouraging the advancement of

knowledge, we can no longer return to the state of subordination and to the magic of collectivism. For him who tasted the fruit of knowledge, the paradise is lost. The harder we try to return to the heroic era of collectivism, the deeper we plunge into a situation defined by the Inquisition, the secret police, and romanticized gangsterism. If we start with suppressing reason and truth, we will arrive at the cruelest violent destruction of all that is human. There is no return to harmonious nature. If we turn back, we will have to go all the way: to the condition of primitive beasts. ... If we dream of returning to our childhood; if we intend to derive our happiness from relying on others; if we are afraid to bear our cross – the cross of humanity, reason, and responsibility; if we lose our courage and escape the charged rhythm of life, then we should stick by our simple selection. We can go back to being wild beasts. But if we want to remain human, we have only one path – one leading to open society. We must enter the unknown, the uncertain, the unsafe, and use our mind to secure stability and freedom for ourselves as best as we can.

Also of interest are observations on the open society made by George Soros, who seems to be developing Popper's ideas further.

Soros believes that people must deem it more important to adopt this or that decision by constitutional means, rather than imposing their ideas on society by other means, such as through one-man decisions or through creating an atmosphere of fear.

Democracy cannot be imposed by decree. Democracy strikingly resembles science. Objectivity of a scientific method is directly linked to its effectiveness. Science uses discovery to break out of the vicious circle; discovery convinces better than an argument. Similarly, democracy requires positive changes in order to justify its existence: a growing economy, intellectual and spiritual stimulation, and a political system that would meet human aspirations better than competing government forms.

This is the main condition for the triumph of democracy: people should have real freedom.

Democracy is the driving force of creativity. However, if society recognizes democracy as an ideal, this may not be enough for its successful progress. Someone must also implement this idea; the leaders must be true to its ideals.

Many scientists, statesmen, and politicians have repeatedly established the superiority of an open society over the closed one. And yet the most convincing evidence is offered by life itself. Since antiquity, human history demonstrates the relation between a society's democratic content and its economic development. This is not an absolute relation, and occasional deviations are possible. Today, no country, whether it is an open or closed society, is isolated from the world outside, so both the interconnectedness and "disturbances" are inevitable.

Stable and solid state machinery is indeed necessary, though not to create a totalitarian regime, but in order to secure democracy and to serve as a guarantee of gained freedom, civil rights, and observance of laws that apply to all citizens without exception.

The democratic state of society is supported and improved by state institutions. Democracy is not a demagogical statement of its leader: "We live under democracy." In the first place, society needs constitutional norms and laws defining the foundation of democratic principles. Yet even that is not enough, since many totalitarian regimes formally adopt basic democratic laws. These laws must "work," i.e., apply to all citizens without exception. One sole exception, one privileged social group, one closed-off area where the laws do not apply, the slightest pressure on the tiniest dissident group operating within the law – any of these creates conditions for the emergence of a totalitarian regime. In fact, totalitarianism has already started.

It is known that a free man is twice as productive as a nonfree one. If labor is wellpaid, the economy is growing healthy in a chain effect. Higher productivity secures a flow of funds into the state budget, and the state uses it wisely to resolve social problems that are inevitable even in the most perfect system.

In the closed society, opposition does not appear to exist, or else exists as a puppet opposition that suits the dictator. This society is seriously sick from inside and is inexorably moving to its doom, for there is no alternative. There is an inherent conflict in each individual, and it is improbable that ten thousand or a hundred thousand or seven million people all thought identically. In a closed society, official statistics often claim that over 90 percent of the public support the regime, sharing the ideas of one man. This claim is completely absurd and a sign of the regime's pathology. With such outward universality of opinion, an open society cannot be created through the efforts of the regime proper, which could be an explosive situation with a tragic outcome for both the dictator and his clique inevitable.

The United States is the most vivid modern example of an open society. It is a community of people with different views, historical experience, national and cultural traditions, religious and political convictions. Here, Buddhists, Hasids, Moslems, Baptists, Evangelical Christians, Catholics, Protestants, and atheists all manage to coexist. One can enumerate indefinitely the diverse convictions held by Americans; with all its problems, this society is a civilized community, whose every member has a right to choose his path without being deprived of the opportunities available to everyone and securely protected by the state within the framework of the law.

Through the analysis of the current international situation, with both democratic and totalitarian regimes developing, George Soros arrives at remarkable conclusions:

- The world is entering a stage of universal disorder.
- Theoretical concepts of both open and closed societies are useful for assessing the modern situation.
- While there is no danger of returning to the Communist past, there is a distinct trend toward economic chaos.
- Newly independent countries are using growing nationalism to bolster statehood.

■ Combined with religious dogmas, nationalism can spread beyond the former Communist world and cause a Christian-Moslem confrontation.

■ Extreme lack of social values in the democratic world leads to indifference and self-absorption, hence the democracies' inability to prevent a wave of nationalist dictatorships and military conflicts they would cause.

These conclusions are largely correct, but I also see substantial simplification caused by the euphoria of the collapse of the Evil Empire. I find the conclusion regarding the impossibility of returning to the Communist past overly optimistic; there is a real danger of a return to Communist ideas in "softer" packaging. The same goes for the real danger of emerging dictatorships in post-Communist countries: such dictatorships are already in existence.

While remarking on the passivity of the official West toward post-Soviet dictatorships, Mr. Soros notes:

> Communism represented the idea of a universal closed society. This idea has failed. There was a small window of opportunity for the idea of a universal open society to take hold. But that would have required the free world's open societies to sponsor that idea. Since an open society is a more advanced form of social organization than a closed society, it is impossible to make this transition in one revolutionary leap without a firm helping hand from the outside.

The Western democracies lacked the vision and this opportunity was lost. The universal closed society has broken down and no new unifying principle has taken its place. Universal ideas generally are in disrepute. People are concerned solely with their own survival, and can be aroused to a common cause only by a real or imagined threat to their collective survival. Unfortunately, such threats are not difficult to generate. One can use ethnic conflicts in order to mobilize people behind the leadership and to create particular closed societies. Milosevic has shown the way, and he has many imitators....

The trouble is that technical assistance is rendered by bureaucracies with all their negative features. Bureaucrats are sometimes very decent, well-intentioned people, but they are confined by rules. We joke inside the foundation that Western aid is the last remnant of a command economy, since it is designed to satisfy the needs of the donors, not the needs of the recipients.

...Even if the West had done everything right, it would take a long, wearying process with many errors. But at least the ex-Communist world would be moving in the right direction. More importantly, Western democracies would be feeling it, too. Western Europe needed Eastern Europe for spiritual, moral, and emotional content.

There is much truth in these bitter words written by a man who has been closely involved in both the idea of the open society and its actual implementation in many former bastions of totalitarianism.

However, such errors were made in other regions of the world as well. Mr. Haggani, Pakistan's former Ambassador in Sri Lanka, in his article "Heritage of Division," spoke of Pakistan's founders' intentions of establishing a democratic state based on Islamic values in the same way as other states that espouse Judeo-Christian values. He wrote:

> Pakistan's main weakness lies in its failures to create and develop democracy. For eleven years of its independence it was ruled by the military, and it is still struggling to build a transitional political system.
>
> The intervention of the military into Pakistan politics was attributed to the public desire to take an active part in the Cold War. Unlike India, who remained unaligned, Pakistan joined US-supported military alliances and allowed the use of its territory for espionage against the Soviet Union. Contrary to Pakistan's expectations, it did little to secure its safety vis-à-vis India. Yet it did give the military a chance to seize power at the time when American leadership was sympathetic towards non-Communist Third World dictators. Under its military leadership, Pakistan also played a key role in US-sponsored operations against the Soviet occupation in Afghanistan, which ultimately and substantially

affected the weakening of the Communist Empire.

Although Pakistan can take pride in its moral opposition to Communism, some Pakistanis feel they have lost the Cold War. The Western support of the military rule harmed democracy. The Afghanistan War resulted in the emergence of well-armed Islamic groups that threaten Pakistan's stability. Finally, part of the weaponry designated to go to Afghanistan ended up in the hands of the Pakistani underworld.

Pakistani founders conceived of a democratic state based on Islamic values, more or less in the same way as Judeo-Christian civilization remains the keystone of the Western democracy. In the times of independence, Islam has been a uniting force for Pakistan. It can remain one, if the currently prevalent intolerance is replaced with an attitude of tolerance towards it.

I see the Western attitude to Islamic values (apart from fundamentalist and extremist ones) as certainly paradoxical. In the United States, a considerable part of the population worships Islam, and this is accepted calmly and reasonably. The situation changes when it comes to dealing with other countries. The West adopts preconceived notions of Islam as antipodal to Western civilization, ignoring that Islam, just like other beliefs, is a part of the world culture, interweaving with other religions. I believe this to be a temporary misunderstanding, eventually to disappear from American for-

141

eign and domestic policy, just like the country has over-come the racial and other contradictions of the past.

Returning to the open society as an inevitable form of civilized commonwealth, I'd like to note the following. Many theorists and practitioners recognize such serious difficulties as the open system's inherent insta-bility and dynamic nature of the economy, its unpredictability, which results in unpredictability of other aspects of society as a whole.

Indeed, in the open society people have to solve many problems on their own. An open society, as Mr. Soros precisely and frankly defines it, is based on the recognition that a man acts on the basis of imperfect knowledge; no one is the ultimate keeper of knowl-edge. Consequently, one should be guided not by dog-matic principles, nonexistent or invented criteria; one should proceed from critical analysis and creative think-ing, which creates the need for state institutions that encourage peaceful coexistence of people with differ-ent principles and interests. As Mr. Soros says:

> We need a democratic form of government
> that observes the transition of power in ac-
> cordance with accepted rules; we need a mar-
> ket economy that secures the return on capi-
> tal and allows us to correct errors; we need
> protection for minorities and respect of mi-
> nority opinions. But most of all, we need the
> protection of the law. Ideologies like Fascism
> and Communism lead to the creation of a
> closed society, where a man is subordinated
> to the collective, the state governs the soci-
> ety, and the state serves the dogma in order

to affirm the universal truth. Such a society has no freedom.

I believe that a man's liberation from slavery and rallying his creative potential toward solving political, economic, philosophical, and personal problems will stimulate his progressive development. On the contrary, adherence to wrong values, a life spent in reliance on the opinions of and support by others, will lead to regression and a return to a tribal, semianimalistic way of life. The challenges of an open society are life-affirming, rather than pernicious. And the role of the state mechanism is dedicated to solving these problems. A member of an open society lives in a real world; he does not dodge difficulties and problems, constantly emerging in various spheres of public life; he solves them creatively in order to achieve his freely selected objectives. A man of the open society is a creator, not a tiny bolt in the state mechanism.

Certainly lily-pure open and closed societies can exist only in theory, but there is a principal difference between theory and practice. According to Soros, the open society recognizes these differences and strives toward a state of balance. The closed society denies these contradictions, and its state can be described as "static unbalanced."

There are inevitable difficulties in the transition from a closed society to an open one. A radical solution of this problem requires systemic changes. If we limit ourselves to such measures as investments aimed at boosting this or that sector of the economy, this may lead – and does – to the emergence of new totalitarian systems featuring attractive facades that conceal the same

143

false content and invented values as did the departed Soviet totalitarianism.

The challenge facing the developed open societies is to prevent a new curve of the totalitarian spiral, to refrain from encouraging the reemergence of dictatorships through indifference or lack of interest. An open society must be able to defend itself; since it is a part of an open system, negative changes in its different components will inevitably affect the stability and progressive development of a democratic society. Mankind must join efforts against the menace of totalitarianism.

Expressing the spirit and ideals of the United States, Thomas Jefferson wrote in the Declaration of Independence:

> We hold these Truths to be self-evident, that all Men are created equal, that they are endowed by their Creator with certain unalienable Rights, that among these are Life, Liberty, and the pursuit of Happiness – that to secure these Rights, Governments are instituted among Men, deriving their just power from the Consent of the Governed, that whenever any form of Government becomes destructive of these ends, it is the right of the People to alter or to abolish it, and to institute new Government, laying its foundation on such principles, and organizing its powers in such form, as to them shall seem most likely to effect their Safety and Happiness.

As President Jefferson stated, "God gave us life, and freedom with it."

In his inauguration speech on January 20, 1997, President Bill Clinton, speaking of prospective development in the 21st century, mentioned problems involved in the development of an open society:

> Times change, and the government must change with them. In the new century we need a new government, and it should be sufficiently modest so that it does not try to solve all of our problems for us, and sufficiently strong so that it supplies tools we need to solve these problems. A smaller government would live within its means and do more while spending less. Yet this government must do more, not less, as it defends our values and interests all over the world, so as to endow Americans with authority to effect real changes in everyday life.

These words ring true to all those who chose to pursue the path of building an open democratic society, whose members can realize their potential and aspirations, while being securely protected and endowed with the authority of a free man of a free land.

2. PARADOXES OF GLOBAL DEMOCRACY

Now that the historic confrontation between the open and the closed societies has resulted in the convincing triumph of the former, it is necessary and useful that all the countries opting for democratic development comprehend the causes of economic power of the developed capitalist powers and the correlation between democracy and economic progress.

The fundamental concepts and features of a modern capitalist society are already outlined in the numerous works of prominent economists and analysts. I will focus on the aspects especially relevant for the countries that have emerged from the totalitarian Soviet desert and are in the transition stage toward the open democratic society. Since the classic texts are well known, I will examine some of the latest Western economical writings.

As society progressed from its simplest forms to the forerunners of highly developed modern democracies, natural factors gradually ceased to dominate the national economy and welfare. At the same time, the human factor grew in importance. At early stages, crafts were passed from generation to generation, or authoritarian fiat dispatched the workforce to accomplish such monumental tasks as building the Egyptian pyramids or reaching Stalin's five-year target figures. These methods did not require substantial participation of professional economists, and economic tasks were resolved by theologians, statesmen, and philosophers: the population had to be clothed, fed, and entertained.

The emergence of "the market system" brought to life a structure based on a simple task: each was to do whatever brought him the most profit. It was at this stage, when optimal economic decisions were sought, that economists moved to the forefront. They had to solve a puzzle: how is society to exist if each member pursues his own good? The emergence of a market economy that replaced the economy based on traditional occupations or authoritarian decisions was the

146

most revolutionary event in modern history. These fundamentally new social relations predated Adam Smith's birth by two centuries.

While his friends and relatives thought Adam Smith to be absentminded, the modern world sees him as a great intellectual and a philosopher-economist of the highest rank. He was born in Scotland in 1723, when merchandise was frequently paid for with nails, for example, rather than with money. According to his biographers, he was kidnapped by the Gypsies when he was four years old. Pursued by his uncle, the Gypsies fled, leaving the boy at the side of the road. Although the biographers sarcastically note that, considering his anecdotal absentmindedness, he would make a poor Gypsy, this fact may well have had a great effect on the future economist. He became a bookworm and pondered things dismissed for centuries by many others. His legacy is comprised in three books: *Theory of Moral Sentiments, An Inquiry into the Nature and Causes of the Wealth of Nations, and Political Justice.*

In the first one, Smith tried to resolve this problem: How is it possible that a man, a creature with pronounced proprietary interests, is able to arrive at moral judgments that seem to overshadow his own interest? He answered that a man sets himself as an independent referee and thus arrives at an objective judgment of an event.

This conclusion was very important for Smith. He understood that he could analyze in depth the world around him and make abstract judgments that would not only explain the relations emerging in the course of work by precisely marking its main elements but also reveal trends and laws that regulate the driving social forces. Adam Smith created an entire world of economic terms and principles that for the first time provided a key to understanding the psychology and essence of the relations among the people participating in work and then exchanging its product. He opened the doors that were closed before and taught lessons that mankind still finds useful.

Behind the appearance of chaos and uncertainty of market relations, Smith saw precise laws and ruling factors. He was the first to recognize that the true wealth of a nation consists in the products consumed by its members. He was the first to pose the following questions: How can a society exist if everyone pursues his own interest? What is the driving force of private production toward satisfying the society's needs? How does a society survive in the free market without authoritarian guidance or conservative traditions?

Smith turned political economy into an elegant body of knowledge and developed important categories of surplus value by suggesting that a product's value should be defined by the profit gained from the capital, the land, and the labor ("classic triad").

Smith and other great economists who followed him discovered that a society based on market relations is not static, but dynamic; it changes constantly and improves itself as it moves through the stages of a dynamic process. Smith's laws of market relations are simple and form a system of "perfect freedom" that nourishes the competition among individual producers, each of whom pursues maximum profit from his goods. This competition is a perfect market regulator by dictating the amount of product that should be produced in a certain time period, its price, its quality, the number of workers needed, and finally the net profit. Smith studied in detail this regulating mechanism in numerous examples from different sectors of his contemporary life. On the basis of his analysis, he concluded that a free market has a self-regulating nature. Thus chaos engenders order, not one imposed by directives and fiats, but one that agrees with active relations among manufacturers, sellers, and consumers. Smith warns: the government should not interfere with the free market, for such interference would be vain and useless; on the contrary, it should promote market improvement with reasonable measures.

Adam Smith was the first to discover the secret of market relations. He did not have the time to say everything, but his theory was followed and improved by such economists as David Ricardo, John Stuart Mill, Henry George, and John Maynard Keynes.

What is the capitalist society today?

First of all, it is a social order in a permanent dynamic state, based upon its own logic, direction, and laws of movement. It is a self-organized process, driven by capital, whose main characteristic consists in creating yet more capital and turning it to production, while it is in turn regulated and driven by the free market.

Modern ideas of the paths of the free market are far more complex than the earlier simplified theories. But the impulse provided by Adam Smith and his followers still generates new ideas that help us understand the market and foresee its future trends.

Classical economic theory presumes that parties in market relations are acting on the basis of perfect knowledge. This is an error. A participant's ideas affect the market, but the reverse is also true: the market affects his ideas as well. As a result of this two-way interaction, the participant can never have perfect knowledge of the market, and the real-life behavior of the market is far more complex than that derived from the assumption of perfect knowledge.

The parties in market relations cannot equate their perception with reality, since they have to take into account the perception of all parties, including themselves. As a result, instead of agreement, we have a certain gap between perception and reality, between intentions and results.

The Soviet totalitarian system was the most comprehensive one, embracing totalitarian rule, a totalitarian economy, a territorial empire, and a totalitarian ideology. The closed nature of the system was enhanced by its complete isolation from the world outside. Everything about it was rigid and inflexible: the Marxist dogma (dominant preconception) and the political system (dominant trend). Therefore, the period of acceleration, when both the preconception and the trend are almost unshakable, is also marked with particular cruelty. This period was in effect under Stalin, especially following the Second World War's ordeals.

Stalin's death was followed by a moment of truth, which found reflection in Khruschev's famous address to the 20th Party Congress. Yet the regime reaffirmed itself, and the twilight era began. The dogma was still bolstered by administrative methods, but it was no longer supported by a universal belief in its justice and unshakability. The system became more rigid. The Party line was changed according to the leader's fancy. Simultaneously, the terror died down, and overall disintegration set in. Central planning was replaced by a system of interministry deals; the "shadow" economy developed, filling the gaps.

The twilight was replaced by stagnation. The inadequacy of the system and the need for radical reforms became obvious. With Gorbachev's ascent to power, alternative development paths emerged; therefore, reforms accelerated disintegration. Economic reform required a political one. With perestroika and glasnost, disintegration entered its final phase; destruction accelerated at a catastrophic pace. The result of this leap-and-fall route was not a transition from a state close to balance to one removed from balance; rather, it was a route from an exceptionally rigid system to another extreme – revolutionary change.

I think – and Western experts, including Soros, agree in various forms – that, as a rule, massive foreign investments end in a debacle. This is what happened when Americans bought European stocks and bonds in late 1950s and early 1960s. The same happened when Americans bought Japanese bonds in 1972. History repeated itself when the Japanese invested abroad in late 1980s and early 1990s.

Financial success is directly linked to the democratic structure of an open society. If money flows directly from the open society into the closed one without substantial structural changes in the latter, this is fraught with serious consequences for both parties. Financial interaction with a society based on totalitarian principles – a half-dictatorship, half-democracy – has no prospect, for sooner or later this trade will go out of control and cause a crisis.

Here is an interesting paradoxical trend of the capitalist path of development: the more powerful the world economy, the more powerful and reliable are small companies. There is a certain aesthetic of the small within the large at work here.

Fritz Schumakher was a prominent champion of small businesses within complex industrial and financial structures. He developed an ethical and philosophical concept of the "small economy," based on Western rational attitudes and Eastern ethical worldview. He bases the advantages of small businesses in the society with hypermodern technology and reasonable solutions of social problems on the following premises:

- Harsh criticism of overregimented systems for their deforming effect on human qualities
- Alarm over aggressive exploitation of natural resources while global ecological problems are ignored
- Criticism of excessive measures in acquisition and consumption of natural resources
- Necessity to introduce limiting principles and develop ethical technologies, or technologies with a "human face"
- Taking into account noneconomic factors while formulating production and consumption policies
- Harmony between moral social criteria and economic development tasks, etc.

These thoughts contain a utopian element, but this is a "healthy" utopia, one based on "conscientious" approaches to strategies and policies of a developed technocratic society.

The above-mentioned global paradox of a developed open-state economy is a steady trend and an objective quality of a politically and economically mature society. The advantage of small forms is observed in all sectors of the economy. They are more profitable, stable, and fitting to human psychology. Their numbers grow every day.

This is how this trend was described by John Nesbitt, a brilliant forecaster of business trends: "The bigger and more open the world economy becomes, the more it is dominated by small and medium-sized companies." Nesbitt notes the following main aspects:

- Removal of trade barriers provided small companies with relatively easy access to the markets that used to be dominated by large corporations whose size afforded them the financial means for cutting through the red tape.
- Computers and other forms of telecommunication provide small companies with access to the newest technologies without the red-tape problems associated with large corporations. This, in turn, provides quick solutions for assembly of new product and implementation of brand-new technological innovations:
- As financial markets become globalized, small and mid-size companies have acquired unparalleled access to raise capital, which ensures their effective participation in investment strategies.
- Small businesses allow high responsiveness to customer needs, production of high-quality goods for the most distinctive taste, faster reaction to the

changes in the marketplace, and new forms of interaction between producing and consuming countries.

■ Small companies provide better opportunity for encouraging their workers' potential by taking into account their psychology and individuality.

Advantages of the small size are evident in all areas of human endeavor: politics, culture, state organization, sports, etc.

According to Nesbitt, structural compartments in businesses shrink in size in order to globalize a world economy more effectively.

This trend – the advantage of small specific forms within a general global framework – demonstrates itself especially vividly in the way ethnic groups are turning back to their ethnic heritage. On the one hand, English is spreading around the world as an international language. On the other hand, national languages and dialects are gaining strength.

Similar trends appear in the formation of new states: soon, there will be a thousand independent democratic states on the planet. One trend is toward political independence of small states; another, toward global economic unions. Large countries, just like large companies, become confederacies of small formations. This agrees with the stable trend of harmonious balance between the general and the specific, the global whole and the unique separate, between the group and the individual.

In addition, according to Carlson and Goldman, we can expect the following global phenomena in the coming decades:

- Accelerated technological innovation and commercial operations on a global scale.
- Introduction of modern technology, in particular disease-prevention methods and telecommunications, with the result of destabilization of less stable societies.
- Stabilization of destabilized societies through universally adopted economic, political, and social measures.
- Complete elimination of Cold War consequences and reorganization in the countries of Eastern Europe and the former Third World.
- Globalization of the world economy. Causes of self-isolation of powerful or backward countries will be eliminated.

These researchers believe that the leading group will still include the United States, Canada, Western Europe, New Zealand, Australia, and Japan. There will be dynamic modernization in South Korea, Taiwan, Thailand, Singapore, Malaysia, Hong Kong, Portugal, some East European countries, Turkey, Israel, Chile, Mexico, Argentina, and South China. Slow development is forecast for former Soviet republics, through most of Latin America, North and South Africa, Indonesia, Vietnam, North Korea, Iran, and the Arab Middle East. Areas of North China, Philippines, Nepal, India, Pakistan are termed as risky. Haiti, Central Africa, Somali, Ethiopia, and Bangladesh will be on the verge of collapse.

3. POST-COLLAPSE DEVELOPMENT
MODELS

Following the collapse of the USSR, the situation in the former Soviet republics can be compared only to that of European countries after the World War II. Then, Europe was saved by the Marshall Plan. Here is a brief description of the plan by the brilliant analyst Stephen Ambrose.

In 1946–47, postwar hardship was heightened by a harsh winter. Heavy snowfall paralyzed factories and construction sites, and millions of people were left without jobs and homes. Practically all transportation came to a standstill. The countries that had survived the ordeal of a war of destruction now had to contend with the natural elements. The Iron Curtain erected by the Soviet Union along the perimeter of its new holdings made it impossible to deliver vital materials and goods via roads connecting East and West Europe. The political atmosphere was explosive, with a looming menace of World War III. The former allies had turned into rivals. The totalitarian regime had seized half Europe and was poised to seize the other half.

In this situation, the United States, which had expended a tremendous effort to destroy Nazism, could not allow Europe to slide under the Communist yoke. They recalled the bitter prewar experience when the divisions and disagreements among European leaders had prevented them from uniting in the face of both brown and red plagues. That, coupled with American post-WWI isolation, accelerated Hitler's adventurous plans.

156

This was why on March 12, 1947, American President Harry Truman declared a new national policy of containment of Communism through providing military aid to Greece and Turkey who were directly threatened. But that was not enough. Democratic European countries were in no less danger. Their situation was underscored by their continuing lack of cohesion and persisting antagonism toward Germany, the former aggressor. In essence, the survival of democratic Europe was in question.

At this critical moment, General George Marshall, whom some called the architect of victory over Fascism, entered the stage. The former troop leader arrived in Moscow in his new capacity of the Secretary of State, in order to develop with the Soviets the plans to rebuild Europe. Originally, he was sincerely interested in working with Moscow. Yet each constructive proposal of his was rejected. He returned to Washington and addressed the nation with a famous phrase: "While the patient is drowning, the physicians are holding counsel."

Marshall, who was in the habit of acting quickly and decisively, set out to develop a far-reaching plan for the reconstructing Europe, which plan was named after him. The general was not a mere administrator, but generated ideas as well. His enthusiasm and energy were unshakable even in that day of widespread suspicions and distrust.

As Marshall set forth his plan, he realized that American taxpayers and Republican conservatives would be lukewarm to it. Therefore, he insisted that the aid should not be a simple pumping of funds, but a mutually profitable operation that would encourage the active rebirth of Europe. Marshall also realized that without American support European countries would be unable to withstand the foreign and domestic Communist threat. He also had to convince not just American statesmen, but the American people – who would shoulder the burden of funding the plan – that the plan was in America's own interest.

This was how Marshall solved this problem with so many aspects. First of all, he consolidated European states. Clearly, they possessed the workforce, the professional managers, the necessary institutions and bureaucracy, the know-how, etc. Therefore, in a joint effort he determined the size of financing for the purchases of raw materials, heavy equipment, fertilizer, machinery, and other hardware. All of this was to be purchased in the United States, which resolved the problem of channeling the money. The European states were oriented toward manufacturing the goods and products that their American partners were interested in. In this way he solved the problem of return on the investment.

In order to overcome internal resistance in the United States proper, the American government launched a powerful propaganda campaign, which involved the most hidebound foes of the plan among the Republicans. The Soviet Government received an offer to participate in the reconstruction of Europe, provided that the Soviets and their satellites opened their markets to Western investment. Professional experts from the target countries were assigned to develop the details of the plan and specific programs. According to

Marshall, the main flow of investment was to be aimed at reviving the private industries, rather than the state sector.

After Stalin occupied Czechoslovakia in February 1948, the well-organized and-realized economic program was complemented by military aid. The Soviet aggression was the final straw that helped resolve the American domestic debate in favor of the Marshall Plan. It was approved by the Senate in a 69-17 vote.

Once the European states overcame their differences, they joined the Brussels Union in order to defend their interests. This later served as a basis for NATO. Thus, military and economic support seemed to complement each other. Although the original amount of requested aid was reduced from $28 to $17 billion, with another cut caused by the Korean War, Marshall's Plan went into effect. As a result, England got $3.2 billion; France, $2.7; Italy, $1.4; West Germany, $1.4; and the Netherlands, $ 1.1. Thirteen other European countries received smaller amounts.

As a result, in a very short period, production and trade levels rose dramatically, though there were no noticeable changes in stabilizing the currencies or raising the living standards. But the main target was achieved: Europe was saved, and so was democracy. In the 1950s, West European economies reached the level where they could maintain a dynamic pace of development without further assistance. While the United States played a historic role in the reconstruction of Europe, the plan was accomplished by the European countries, motivated by their own welfare. Thus, the Marshall Plan was effective not only from the point of view of supplying food, goods, and materials, but also, just as importantly, from the point of view of correct ideas and responsible leadership.

But its most important feature was that the financial aid was accompanied with the true democratization of the countries; moreover, the factor of openness and real democracy was the original precondition for the plan.

By December 1951, the plan was completed.

I went into detail on the Marshall Plan in order to return to the idea that the establishment of the open society is possible only under these conditions: democratic infrastructure, public acceptance of the democratic idea, and active and conscious public participation in the process.

There are other ways to solve the numerous economic problems in the transition to an open society. Here are some examples.

Chile. As a result of complicated events, power is assumed by General Augusto Pinochet. The 1980 plebiscite, carefully rehearsed and controlled by the military, adopts the Constitution which leaves Pinochet in power until 1989 with a possible renewal of his mandate. The regime is widely criticized abroad for human rights violations. The Catholic Church condemns the military rule, accusing the secret police of torture and trying to draw public attention to the condition of the poor. Pinochet starts his rule in a typical dictatorial way, in the worst authoritarian scenario.

The abrupt economic fall of 1982–84, with the depression of 1983–84, brings about the discontent of the middle class, the workers, and the poor. The resistance to the regime grows, and it appears that the days of the dictator are numbered. In 1986, there is an attempt on Pinochet's life. These events force Pinochet to turn for help to a group of economists who graduated from Chicago University's School of Economics and invite them to put their knowledge of the free market into practice. They would work autonomously, without supervision, pursuing one objective: dragging the country out of the economic abyss.

"The Chicago Boys," as they were called, were denounced and ridiculed for their consent to work for the dictator. Later, this invitation turned out to be a crucial point in the rise of the economy. They realized that Chilean capitalism was not a market variety, but rather a rigid monopolistic system where punishingly high tariffs and the government's subsidies for local companies made attracting foreign capital a dubious proposal. Hence, they started pushing through the reforms aimed at creating a free market.

The results did not show right away. These events took place against the background of depression and austere economic regimes all over Latin America. However, soon the shift started, especially when a young technocrat named Hernan Büchi was appointed the Minister of Finance in 1985. This appointment marked the beginning of the revival. Büchi's strategy was to create financial conditions for stable export growth and reorganize the structure of the export sector. By 1989, rigid control over public expenditures, periodic devaluation, and encouragement of public savings and foreign investment gradually reduced inflation to 12 percent – the lowest in Latin America in many years. The sale of debts to foreign investors in exchange for shares in industrial enterprises reduced the national debt by $4 billion. While previously copper was Chile's main export, now its share fell from 70 percent in 1973 to 45 percent in 1989. Exports became more varied through the development of other areas: farming, fishing, and lumber industry. New markets for these exports opened up in the Far East, in Australia, and in North America. In 1971 Chile exported 412 products to 58 countries, but by 1988 the numbers went up to 1,343 products to 112 countries. From 1985 to 1988 the Chilean economy grew by 5 to 6 percent a year.

In September 1988, a few weeks before the next plebiscite, the conservative paper *El Mercurio* wrote admiringly: "Good-bye, Latin America. No longer do we look up to Argentine or Brazil as examples for emulation. On the contrary, our task is to reach the living conditions of Australia, New Zealand, or Taiwan."

As a result of the plebiscite, the general lost power. Paradoxically, in the midst of chaos, the public wanted the general, while in a free country he was no longer needed. Did the general suspect this outcome? Do other generals have similar suspicions? Are they capable of emulating Pinochet and making a timely change: first to eliminate Communist totalitarianism, then give broad authority to professional economists and finally – which could be his worthiest act – retire from the political arena and make room for democracy.

Let us go across the Andes to *Argentina* in the late 1980s. After a series of terrorist acts, Carlos Menem, a Peronist candidate, is elected President on a platform of nationalistic slogans and populist appeals to pay com-

162

pensation for skyrocketing prices. Several months prior to his election the inflation went up to 28,000 percent. The fate of Argentina depended on Menem's ability to recreate a consensus on the methods of overcoming economic difficulties

To everyone's surprise, Menem began working for this consensus with a radical program of economic reconstruction: reducing state expenditures and bureaucratic staff, privatizing money-losing state companies and opening the economy for foreign investment. He continued his neoliberal policy, but as the Peronist movement fell apart and militant union leaders stepped up their resistance, he was faced with the danger of hyperinflation and growing foreign debt. Besides, the democratic system was threatened by the military–hence, bloodshed. If Menem could make industry and agriculture economically competitive in the world markets, Argentina could make an economic recovery, and democratic movement would be safe from danger.

Bangladesh in the1970s and1980s. After getting a degree in economics in the United States, Muhammad Yunus came back home to face misery and degradation. An energetic and enterprising person, he had an idea of boosting economic activity in the lowest economic strata by offering small credits for commercially viable activity, however small the profit. Despite pessimistic predictions, Yunus's bank was successful. As the poor obtained aid, they not only made gains in business, but helped improve the society at large.

Yunus's example, amazing for its moral quality, is a good example of revival of human spirit in the areas of society where it seems to have been ruled out.

Muhammad Yunus said optimistically, "If we could achieve this, we can lay down a foundation for the world free of poverty. I am awaiting the day when our children and grandchildren will have to go to a museum in order to see what misery used to be like. We can make it happen. Let's do it."

These are amazing examples. They are striking turns in human fate. They truly show that a creative, dynamic person can achieve incredible results despite resistance and indifference.

Yet the following stages are inevitable in transition to an open society:

- Formation of an open-society infrastructure with wide public participation in creating a democratic state bureaucracy in keeping with constitutional norms
- Investment policy emphasizing small-sized companies in a multiprofile national economy while attracting the investment and know-how from civilized countries
- Solution of "nonprofit" environmental problems based on the experience of civilized countries
- Renaissance of national culture on the basis of historical heritage and national cultural and spiritual values
- Participation in international economic, scientific, cultural, environmental, educational, and other programs.

164

Chapter Four

DEMOCRACY
AND AZERBAIJAN

1. ADDITIONAL TOUCHES TO
THE PICTURE OF THE POST-SOVIET DICTATOR

I have paid enough attention to various dictators in the second chapter of this book. Yet I did not write enough about post-Soviet dictators. Although their principles are absolutely identical with those of their predecessors, there are certain distinct characteristics, mostly in appearance rather than substance: they have to adjust their style to the spirit of the time. Therefore, I will add a few extra touches; but it is not my purpose to intrigue or amuse the reader. The only reactions these touches evoke in me are stress and disgust. *My objective is to help those people who have short memories, or are fearful, or are vulnerable to hypnosis – to help them avoid self-deception as well deception of others. Because the consequences are too sad, because the wounds are still raw, because time has been lost, it is criminal to lose any more time.*

Following in the footsteps of Soviet or pro-Soviet dictators, all subsequent dictators, fully conversant in intrigues and dirty tricks, assume power and instantly surround themselves with petty characters for whom such notions as "conscience," "honor," and "morals" are highly abstract. The main occupation of these court jesters could be called competitive praise, as they vie in singing paeans to the dictator's "great deeds." Although each of them is busy in his narrow "field," they seriously compete as to who will display the most exaltation in contributing to the "holy" cause of glorifying the dictator. Since "there is an opinion," as they put it, that greatness is an absolute substance that neither grows nor wanes and simply changes its appearance, their search for biographical facts that would confirm the dictator's brilliance never stops – just like the search for the Abominable Snowman.

Their diligence reaches absurd extremes.

Let us say that a child's cry at the moment of birth is a sine qua non of normal (perhaps not always) development. However, a young genius (a dictator in his infancy) could not do something like that. If he was hungry, he would let it be known by turning his intelligent and a tad stern gaze toward his mother. By six months he was hopping about merrily, by nine he was talking up a storm, and in the fifth grade he was explaining the latest methods of solving a problem to his stunned teachers. At about the same time he made his mark in scientific research, and by the age of fifteen or sixteen he was a perfectly mature gentleman who, having barely started in his first job, was already advising the head of state. His glorifiers portray him as a wise and experienced politician, almost a Talleyrand (perhaps even greater), who as a youth advised Stalin and

Roosevelt at the same time; a national leader of unsurpassed authority whose advice is sought on the phone by all the world leaders, from Bill Clinton to the Dalai Lama. He is a great peacemaker and warrior, an expert in sophisticated machinery, beer brewing, botanics, in all genres and styles of art and music, to say nothing of shepherding, beekeeping, and genetic engineering. Each "court artist" adds a few brushes of his own to the portrait of this leader, and never forgets to mention his modesty and ascetic lifestyle.

Poets and artists, scientists and workers, shepherds from remote villages, and kindergarten teachers and their wards – everybody tries to put in his two cents' worth of praise. When the portrait is ready, the apogee of popular recognition has been reached.

All the post-Soviet dictators have one thing in common: their personal career is more important than the nation, their friends and relatives, all taken together. There is nothing they will not do for the career, for seizing power and holding on to it – they will lie, slander, betray their country and friends. As time passes, the dictator comes to believe in his own brilliance and infallibility; he is no longer content with standard praise, it no longer suffices, it no longer fully reveals his grandeur. Finally, the choir of flattery and lies is joined by another voice – the dictator's own. This is his moral nadir.

From that point on, his cult snowballs, with no reasonable limit. There's a totalitarian state where they have cut the wooden or granite heads off the old Lenin statues and attached those of the new leader. In another state, as totalitarian, excerpts from the leader's speeches are published in gold-etched binding, in the best tradition of Mao's Red Book. Yet another, like Buddha or dancing Shiva, receives his worshippers' offerings.

For the sake of justice, I'll admit that no dictator ever has avoided the mentioned final stage. Shortly before his death, Stalin said to his colleagues at the Central Committee Presidium: "What will you do after I'm gone? You're a bunch of blind kittens."

As was to be expected, all the members of the Presidium unanimously agreed and each affirmed that he would gladly give up the rest of his life to extend Comrade Stalin's days, because without him they – "the blind kittens" – would be indeed at a loss as to what to do.

This episode is filled with the dictator's amour-propre and tragedy. A horrible tragedy befell 250 million people whose lives fell in the hands of "the blind kittens."

When a dictator surrounds himself with people capable of licking his boots any time, any place (their personal qualities are unimportant; what is important is their ability to "understand" the leader's greatness) whom he consequently scorns (isn't it ironic?), this is the tyrant's personal tragedy. Barely had "the blind kittens" dropped Stalin's still-warm body into the tomb than they relieved the dictator's son of all his high positions and tore his numerous awards off his chest. Ten years later they would pretty much execute him, driving him to delirium tremens – typical of a totalitarian regime. His daughter was tossed out of her Kremlin apartment just as the funeral was coming to an end and later left without means of subsistence. Five or six months later, Stalin's closest allies were executed, and the leader himself, worshipped for three decades by Communist atheists, was criticized so harshly he must have turned in his grave more than once.

Eventually, rejecting the god they had created, his former allies dragged the body out of the tomb, danced a joyous dance over the mummy, and burned it in the Red Square to the mob's applause.

Later on, this would befall them, too.

On February 25, 1956, in his famous speech before the 20th Party Congress, Nikita Khruschev said:

> After Stalin's death, the Party's Central Committee has taken a rigorous unfailing course aimed at explaining that Marxism and Leninism reject the glorification of one person and turning him into a superman endowed with superhuman qualities – like a God. This person is presumed to know everything, see everything, think for everybody, do everything: he is infallible. This notion about a certain person – about Stalin – has been cultivated in our country for many years. Right now we are talking about something that's of enormous import for the Party's present and future – we are talking about how the cult of personality gradually emerged, about a number of particularly striking perversions of Party principles, Party democracy, and revolutionary legality.
>
> He [Stalin] would not employ conviction, explication, patient work with people. What

he did was to impose his orders and demand that the people submit to his opinion unconditionally. Whoever resisted or attempted to prove his viewpoint was doomed to be expelled from leadership with subsequent moral and physical elimination.

These revelations did not help avoiding later repressions, when protests against the regime were suppressed by all means available, up to airplanes and tanks, when dissidents were rotting in the same camps and prisons where victims of Stalinist tyranny used to be held.

Let us return to post-Soviet dictators, and another self-aggrandizing detail. As a rule, this takes place against the background of humiliation, of reducing to nothing the role of other people – in essence, of the entire nation. In the ecstasy of self-affirmation the dictator abandons the frayed slogan, *The Government Owes It to the People*, for a new one, both blasphemous and nonsensical: *The People Owe It to the Leader*. (By now they have forgotten that the naive people had once elected the Leader unanimously, picking him from nowhere, and that he had sworn loyalty and responsibility to the people on the Bible or the Koran.) This is typical of newly formed totalitarian regimes. No opposition will ever ask: what is this debt, what does it amount to, and when is it due?

Sooner or later, people return their debts. The end of every tyrant is a foregone conclusion and is dictated by general social principles. Of course, it is a tragedy of an individual as well. Perhaps we would not be focusing on it as much if it did not exist next to the tragedy of the people; and the scenario for that tragedy is penned by the dictator who steers the totalitarian ship of state.

Post-Soviet totalitarian regimes pave the way to flourishing corruption and bribery. Wherever you have privileged groups who do not obey the general laws, you have conditions for corruption and bribery.

The Soviet totalitarian regime, based on Marxist-Leninist ideology, was merciless toward these phenomena. A twenty-kopeck bribery was enough to have an official executed. A Marxist-bred regime would not allow for such "lapses" in a perfect Communist society. After Stalin's death, the Soviet empire that had existed for thirty-eight years according to Lenin–Stalin theories burst at the seams. The drive to reach this imaginary idealized society fell slack, and corruption picked up pace, especially after the 1960s.

From time to time, the officialdom resisted this indecency, and corruption and bribery were still being recognized as anomalies. After the final collapse of the empire, in the new post-Soviet republics, these have become an element of national policy, as legitimate as taxes flowing into the treasury. The shadow economy adopted a clear-cut pyramidal structure that embraced all government, with the dictator at the top of the pyramid.

The laws of pyramid state policy are even harsher. If a state budget allows for shortages, the budget of a shadow economy must be replenished constantly and be topped off, too. The most striking aspect is the changing size of the budget. There's one iron-clad principle at work here: if one has a chance to exact a certain amount, it means one can always exact more. As a result, the people's lives get worse from day to day, and will get even worse to a yet greater degree. The reason is that a fortune derived from corruption and bribery has one source only – the workingman's pocket. There's simply nothing else.

But the pyramid goes on. The contracts signed today are nothing else but the robbery of the generations to emerge a hundred years from now. Thus, a small group robbing the people through bribery and corruption becomes a force that eliminates, morally and physically, anyone who speaks out against the regime. This force takes the ugliest shapes.

Here is another attribute that no dictator would be caught without – popular applause.

One applauds a dictator always standing, always holding one's breath.

Applause starts on cue: it begins unanimously and ends unanimously. Specially designated claquers cry out admiration for the leader.

Frightened, people applaud louder and faster. Each tries to outapplaud his neighbor. The dictator is content: at this moment he sincerely believes in his genius, his immortality.

Applause has been heard in our country for 70 years. But who will ask people – what are you applauding? Your own tragedy, the tragedy of your children and grandchildren, the tragedy of the future generations who will curse those who have doomed them to a life of debt, an existence without hope, without a gulp of freedom?

People: how long will you keep applauding?

Behind this applause lies total silence. As our famous poet Vagif Samedoglu wrote, "There are many languages one can learn and speak. But what difference does it make in what country and in what language you keep silent?"

Here is another typical touch of dictatorship: building more jails. The old ones, inherited from the Czar, are packed; and the number of potential opponents is great. If a schoolteacher cannot live on his largely symbolic salary, if a retiree is swelling with hunger – never mind, they've lived through worse. Let us build a small jail instead, then another, bigger one; and so on, till the whole country turns into one big jail.

In the meantime we can restore an old church or build a new one, and then hold a service in all possible versions in all possible places: Jerusalem, Moscow, the Vatican. That's one way to have your sins redeemed. God will forgive.

Naturally, a dictator cannot perform his evil deeds single-handedly, so he has to recruit numerous henchmen – state officials, law enforcement, part of the intelligentsia – who thus become his partners in crime.

Why does he need that?

The officials who participate in the dictator's crimes become more obedient and faceless. In order to retain their offices and privileges, unavailable to common folks, they turn into a gang prepared to commit any crime. Also, aware of popular anger, they will try to prolong the dictatorship by all means even after the dictator is gone – and try to find a new one.

Truly, as the dictator creates his system, he follows the logic of all dictators, present and past – horrific architects of an obedient society. And yet their intentions never come to full fruition, and the society always finds resources to resist following the blueprint created by the ruler's inhuman brain.

The fate of the henchmen is no better than that of the tyrant. Even if a new dictator comes along, they are either eliminated or publicly condemned.

History has many lessons. Those who embarked on the path of crime against their own people should learn these lessons and cease and desist. As the proverb says, Nothing wrong in turning off the wrong path. If they don't do so, they will be looking at a personal tragedy.

This is the paradox: normally, no less than 70 percent of state officials and law enforcement are honest, decent people, who share the aspirations of their country. However, in reality, once they are caught in the net of a predatory leader, they will surrender their free will and be guided by their survival instinct. Thus, history teaches us, they will seal their doom.

In the name of holding on to power, a dictator will stoop to anything, never burdening himself with thoughts of his country. Nor will he bother with thoughts of people, their prosperity, their independence. For the sake of power, a dictator will join forces with a powerful neighbor and sell out his people's independence, while another will sell off its wealth, which belongs not only to the current generation, but to at least five or six following. Yet another one, while faking a "balanced" foreign policy ("you're good, he's good, and so I'm good, too"), deliberately sacrifices his national interests so long as he remains in power. Yet another one will do all of the above.

Totalitarian regimes leave unhealing scars on their land and in people's souls. The harsher the regime, the harder the transition to democracy. In such countries as Rumania and Bulgaria, where the regimes were especially rigid, the transition to an open society is going slowly and painfully, in the constant struggle with other country members of the former Warsaw Treaty. Their natural resources are no help.

In the USSR, totalitarianism was at its most liberal in the Baltic countries and at its most rigid in Central Asia and in Azerbaijan. The continuation of totalitarianism after the collapse of the Soviet Union is especially fraught with danger in this transition period, when all material and spiritual connections have been weakened. This danger is far greater than a natural catastrophe like a volcano eruption or an earthquake measuring 12 on the Richter scale. By crippling people's souls, totalitarianism leads to a national catastrophe.

Today's totalitarianism means an aggression against the free spirit and the aspirations for freedom and independence that people have cherished throughout their struggle. It means usurpation of every citizen's spiritual and material values; hence, resisting it is everybody's duty regarding the coming generations and their own conscience.

This struggle for democracy must bring together workers and intellectuals, agricultural engineers and students, retirees and housemaids. No one can afford to stay away, for their country is in danger, for this is about their children and grandchildren and great-grandchildren. This is about the destiny of a nation that has been once imprisoned in a totalitarian regime.

True, we all can throw up our hands: "What can I do by myself?" But this is the kind of sentiment that we have to squeeze out of our slavish minds. The great Azerbaijani poet Mamed Araz wrote these words that sound like a curse to this day:

You dodged the bullet, and so did I
But our Motherland got it in the heart.

Unfortunately, this philosophy is not confined to those who experienced the misery of totalitarianism. Through the years of the Soviet regime, since the emergence of the Bolshevik threat, the civilized world has been taking a wait-and-see attitude.

As trade developed in the past 400 years, fewer countries are isolated from the world. No modern state can survive on its own. Economic integration leads to a political one: more countries emerge with the same political system, laws are being adopted that agree with international ones and those of other countries, new international organizations are being established.

The civilized world recognizes the inviolability of state borders, the principle of noninterference in other states' domestic affairs, the observance of human rights, freedom of expression and conscience. The international community cannot remain indifferent to the countries who fail to recognize these principles.

However, in reality, in many countries power is grabbed by a bunch of dictators who doom their people to repression. Aided by the Soviet Union, the world has sprouted innumerable totalitarian regimes: Nicaragua, Cuba, Angola, Ethiopia, North Korea, Vietnam, China, Cambodia, Laos, Libya, Hungary, Czechoslovakia, Rumania, Bulgaria – the list can go on. Communism had a hand in the fascist triumph in Germany and Italy.

How did the civilized world resist this plague? Was there noticeable political pressure? Were material resources used? They did not go beyond statements of condemnation. And we all know disaster befell millions of people as a result.

After the 1917 Bolshevik coup, a group of Czarist generals fought hard against the new rulers. Yet, instead of aiding the patriots in ridding their country of the plague, the West traded with the Bolsheviks, trying to negotiate their future stakes. As a result, Lenin and his government created an unparalleled totalitarian regime, where human rights were on a par with those of animals, and the civilized world got an adversary for the next seventy years.

The United States played a special role in bolstering the political and economic power of Lenin's and Stalin's governments. It was advanced American technology and equipment that enabled Stalin to industrialize Russia in 1922–33, and the politics of compromise during and after World War II created conditions for the spread of Socialism throughout the world.

What did the West gain and lose as a result of playing footsie with the USSR?

Aiming for quick and easy profits in the 1930s, Western countries handed over their advanced technology, which enabled the USSR to industrialize, while they found themselves pushed out in 1933. They lost both their investments and any hope for future profits.

First they refused to help the Czarist generals, and then spent the subsequent decades in fear of Soviet aggression, spending colossal moral and material resources. Who will ever add up these numbers?

Although the West went into the Cold War, more active engagement occurred with President Reagan, who had the courage to declare the USSR "The Evil Empire." How much was spent, before that moment and after, to preserve "Solidarity" alone? How much intellectual energy was spent on exposing "the Evil Empire"? How much was spent on ruining the Communist economy by dragging it into the space and nuclear race? Hundreds of billions of dollars. Certainly millions times more than it would have taken to choke the monster in its embryo stage.

It is said that when Bismarck was shown a Communist program, he called it interesting, noted its good sides, and then said, "All we need to do now is to find a miserable country that would test this monstrous project."

Well, they found this country, and the test was held on a colossal scale, on culturally and historically diverse nations. Was the purpose of the test to demonstrate that you cannot provide for the earth's growing population by standard means; that you need wars and other methods of eliminating people in order to match population numbers with food production? But, as mentioned above, our planet can perfectly well provide for its inhabitants, even for a population a hundred times greater than today. Today, mankind faces little threat of starvation, especially with science discovering yet new ways of dealing with it.

On many occasions the United States and Western Europe, guided by incomprehensible calculations, supported totalitarian regimes or looked the other way, missing many opportunities of helping democratic movements.

Such examples include the support of the Shah's regime in Iran, the generals in Pakistan and Latin America. As a rule, this ended in a failure. If early on, instead of propping up the Shah's regime, the United States would have promoted democratic institutions in Iran, the country would not have the problems it has now. Thank God, the latest presidential elections were held democratically, which gives hope that things will change for the better in this beautiful country that has so much in common with my land.

Why am I drawing attention to these events of the recent past? Because similar mistakes are being repeated today. Because the minds of politicians and economists are still befogged by short-range considerations.

Having been assured that the Soviet collapse is a fact, Western countries are practically ignoring the issue of what kind of regimes are emerging in the new countries. Their priority is to establish an area of calm and stability; they are not concerned if these are following in the footsteps of the Gulag, the way it was described by Solzhenitsyn. Ironically, Western democracies are more attracted to totalitarian regimes in the former republics, for regimes like these secure an appearance of peace devoid of rallies and demonstrations. The utilitarian approach suggests that it is more convenient to deal with one boss who would make decisions for the entire nation, including the generations to come. Such a policy leads to bolster the images of the dictators who only yesterday occupied Party thrones and who today are trying to pass themselves off as Democrats. Such a policy will once again create favorable conditions for replacing an ideology of freedom and reason with one of fear and military subordination.

Gentlemen! You are on the verge of making another historic mistake. First of all, the chance of the revival of empire is real, and the recent events in Belarus confirm it. Could this have taken place immediately after the collapse of the USSR, or after Lukashenko was elected President? No: he needed time to revive a totalitarian regime. This is why he, with the whole world watching, eliminated his opposition, had the members of parliament beaten up, forced an election of new obedient deputies, and only then made himself a sole dictator. Could he have succeeded in a democracy? No. Could this have happened if democrats were in the majority in the Russian Duma? No, again.

After the collapse, Russia has been advancing toward an open democratic society more consistently than the other republics. Despite the latest Communist victory, both parliamentary and presidential elections were held, according to international observers, in keeping with democratic and constitutional norms.

These were followed by elections in other independent countries, former Soviet republics. In many, democratic norms were violated; the results were falsified; open, sometimes violent, pressure was exercised on voters; occasional scuffles were recorded. This was noted by all international observers – except the Russian ones, who consistently declared the elections legitimate, even when violations were blatant.

How come the Russian Federation, having chosen a democratic path for itself, is supporting totalitarian regimes in former republics? Does it sympathize with them – and it knows them full well for what they are? Of course not. But once a dictator feels his regime shaking, he will not hesitate to "reunite" with Russia, which will result in a new, somewhat looser Empire. As for popular opinion, sacrifices, principles of independence and democracy – all of these will once again be ignored. Prior to creating the USSR, the Bolsheviks had established totalitarian regimes in the independent states – Azerbaijan, Georgia, Ukraine, and others – and only then united them into an empire.

For the moment, all post-Soviet dictators without exception are exhorting their cadres to create a democratic image for both domestic and foreign consumption. The dictator himself is depicted as the only guarantor of this "democracy."

We've seen that before.

Today, no one needs to be convinced that there was but one country where democracy was wholly absent as a concept (they even had an expression, "so-called democracy"), and it was the Soviet Union.

Nonetheless, from the moment the monster was born, the program of deluding the public was implemented with a great deal of energy. Debates within the Bolshevik government under Lenin, praise of Stalin's Constitution – which took millions of tons of paper to print, and in a starving country, too! – all of these constituted a well-planned strategy. Meanwhile, the dictator was going out of his way to seduce as many naïfs as possible – not just his own citizens, but foreigners as well. Stalin allowed international observers to the show trials of 1937–38; Hitler held the Olympics in 1936 –

these examples show how much a dictator would "sacrifice" for the sake of his propaganda. Unfortunately, they worked: with all the Nazi crimes, the world not only looked the other way but in fact justified the Nazi regime with statements that Hitler's danger to Europe was "exaggerated."

If early in the history of the "barracks Socialism" only a Soviet man could sing _I do not know of any other country where a man breathes so freely_, soon, through the efforts of Stalin and his flunkeys to reveal "lies and inventions" about the Soviets, hundreds of famous Western journalists, scientists, writers, and public figures unanimously expressed support for the Soviet regime and confidence that soon the world would emulate this country as the true champion of freedom and democracy. This took place at the height of Communist terror.

Little has changed in the nature of totalitarianism today; the more cruel the regime, the harder it tries to prove its democratic nature to the world. Soon, it is supported not just by individual scientists, writers, and public figures, but entire organizations – the International Monetary Fund, the World Bank, the Bank for Reconstruction and Development, etc. – who emerged in the world arena relatively recently, but have already gained great successes. While providing small credits, they gradually take over the financial and macroeconomic control of the country, as they misinform the world public of political and economic reforms being implemented. As they in fact conspire with the dictator, they fabricate a democratic image for a totalitarian regime. "Control of the economy in exchange for a democratic image" – this is the essence of the trade-off.

Thus, genuine independence is a fiction, while the public is being pushed away from running the country for years to come. There are dozens of countries who have surrendered their independence to the International Monetary Fund and the World Bank. Naturally, this policy is being conducted in the guise of "public interest and welfare." For the sake of this "interest." millions of human lives come to ruin, and entire generations are doomed to a life of hopeless slavery.

What motivates these "protectors" of people's interests? As a rule, they declare that

■ What you need now is stability, not democracy.

■ There's no rush: you will have democracy one day. It took the civilized world hundreds of years to gain it.

■ Finally, the most cynical statement: installing democratic institutions is not in our national interest, since it will lead to reforms, which you may need, but which are not good for us. It is more convenient to deal, and easier to find a common language, with a dictator.

Do these "great" statesmen realize their responsibility for the future? Or does the blood spilled by totalitarian regimes with their abettance and support cover their eyes and blind them to future catastrophes? They should look at the recent past – and shudder as they do.

Let us turn to the dry statistics of the most totalitarian regime of this century – the Soviet Union. In 1918–30, 3 to 4 million people were physically eliminated. In 1930–40, 5 million were starved to death as a deliberate state policy, and 8 million perished in purges. In World War II, the Soviet Union lost 30 million lives, with 10 million missing in action, while the losses of the rest of the world, including Germany, came up to 20 million. In 1945–53, about 8 million were executed and exiled, among them Soviet Army POWs, who were declared "enemies of the people." Even after Stalin, in the years of demagogic appeals to "catch up with and outdo America," of "mature Socialism" and "Socialism with a human face," tens of millions of people encountered the repressive mechanism of the state in one form or another. The number of patients in psychiatric asylums grew steadily; the whole country turned into an asylum.

If against this nightmarish background the absolute number of Azerbaijani victims seems to "fade," this does not lessen the tragedy, which in a certain way is even greater. Under Stalin's regime, 400,000 Azerbaijanis perished, and 300,000 died in WWII, which comes to 20 percent of a 3 million population. It is no lesser tragic that the Azerbaijani intelligentsia, which emerged at the turn of the century as a result of the efforts of oil tycoons, was physically wiped out. They were persecuted for any reason: Pan-Turkism, "pseudoscientific" theories in natural sciences, and simply for independent thinking. The machine of state terror did such a thorough job of purging the nation of its intelligentsia that, when Khruschev's "thaw" gave rise to the dissident movement in Russia, in Azerbaijan it was practically nonexistent. As a result of Stalin's crushing blow, followed by continuous pressure on the Azerbaijan psyche, even now politics are being discussed in a whisper, and only with the most trusted

184

people. No one does it over the phone, since every-body is convinced his line is bugged.

People ready to sacrifice their lives in the name of a change for the better have been and are persecuted. This is being done by the dirtiest, most nefarious meth-ods, hoping that the prey will break down; if he does not, the heat is applied to his close family, and then the entire family, however extended, is wiped out. Conse-quently, in many former republics it is so hard to find relatives of those who 50 or 70 years ago comprised the country's intellectual elite.

Modern-day dictators do not resort to terror against their own citizens. In some places, even death sentences are being commuted. Yet the jails are filled with people who are "inconvenient" for the regime, with their rela-tives, while "unnecessary" people are being eliminated by hired killers.

As long as the regime exists, the inmates of post-Soviet prisons are doomed. Death sentences are com-muted to yet crueler punishment, which dooms the victim to a slower and painful death. The jailers inher-ited their arsenal from Stalin's regime: some victims, already driven to insanity by torture, are not even trans-ferred to a psychiatric unit and are being left in regular jail. Torture is being used to obtain evidence necessary for hammering together a case that can be used at any time against yet another "unnecessary" citizen.

One of the tasks is the elimination of the middle class, regarded as the main threat to the regime, and eliminating the very conditions for its future emergence. The reason is that organized protests of the middle class are much more dangerous than a riot of a hungry mob. Consequently, a totalitarian regime tries to reduce the social structure to two classes: a privileged group that makes up 1 or 2 percent of the population, and the rest, 98 to 99 percent, starved and impoverished in comparison with the life of the elite.

The regime nourishes the cult of one "family" (not in a blood sense), whose members comprise the privileged class. This family is a closed clan, based on corruption, expropriation of state property, and extortion. The rest of the population is barred from its ranks. The logic is simple: a "stranger" with even a little money might turn his means against the "family." Therefore, whatever the "family" deems as "excessive means" is being expropriated, while the people are assigned one function – indentured service to their masters.

Some will undoubtedly reproach me for subjectivity, bias, even treason of the interests of the Azerbaijani people. As an argument, they will cite Khanysh-kishi with his innumerable sheep herds and endless acres of land. You must be blind, they'll say, to ignore achievements of common people like him. But we, former Soviet citizens, have many past examples of totalitarian propaganda – Stakhanov, for example. We won't buy this argument.

Six years of Azerbaijan independence have not seen a single prominent Azerbaijan company emerge. To the contrary, the people who started out at the dawn of perestroika participating in many financial projects on the national (Soviet) level are by now wiped out. Thousands of young Azerbaijani businessmen and entrepreneurs, men of high intellectual potential, have left the country for lack of opportunity.

Why? By now the whole world can see that national development and prosperity are least of all related to the natural resources, which have never made a single nation happy. The main wealth of a nation is its intellectual potential. However, the higher the intellectual level of the population, the higher the numbers of intellectuals, the more of a threat they are for the totalitarian regime. Therefore, ridding the country of these people is the most important task of the regime, for their absence facilitates the appropriation of the national wealth and the transformation of the people into an obedient mass.

There is a ridiculous argument that the people themselves are the problem, that some nations will not live and develop normally under any circumstances. If so, how come Turkey, which moved from a military regime to democracy in 1982, managed to make such a leap in the next five to six years? Today, Turkish companies can be found all over the world, and the number of transcontinental Turkish corporations is growing steadily.

How come we, Azerbaijanis, Turkomans, Uzbeks, Kazakhs, and Kyrgyzes cannot achieve the same? The difference lies not in the people's lack of ability, but in the political system.

It is sometimes said that people deserve the government they have elected – that the people are themselves to blame for their troubles. It is also said that democracy is an optimal form of government for some nations due to their tradition, geographical location, environment, the government in the neighboring countries. These nations can be happy only with democracy, for it is an organic part of their national character. At the same time, other nations do not accept democracy, for it leads to chaos, degradation, and economic deterioration; this is a pet theory of demagogical dictators.

You are wrong, gentlemen, I say to those who have already managed to inculcate a pessimistic view of democracy in their nations (and some Western politicians who share this view). This theory is essentially antihuman, and designed to forgive a dictator's sins and justify his crimes and despotism.

I would like to illustrate my point with two vivid examples from modern history: Germany and Korea.

Through their misfortune, hardworking, disciplined German people were divided into two states: East and West. They became two diametrically opposite states. Under the so-called developed Socialism, the East Germans ruined their economy and lost many centuries of civilized tradition. At the same time, the West evolved into an open democratic society, with the highest levels of political and economic development.

Korea, divided into North and South, is a similar story. Under a totalitarian yoke the North turned into an Orwellian "Animal Farm," while the South evolved according to the principles of the free world and has become one of the world's most developed and civilized countries.

In the wake of the collapse of 1991, each newly independent state had a more or less equal chance. How did they use it? Today in the Baltic republics the living standards are ten times higher than in Azerbaijan, despite their absolute lack of natural resources; Russia's living standards are eight times higher, too. As for other republics, their respective living conditions are related to their democracy levels. For example, Azerbaijan is second from the bottom in this table, and Turkmenistan is the third, despite both countries' extraordinary natural resources.

Some Western politicians developed a classical formula that justifies collaboration with totalitarian regimes. Basically, it goes like this: If we put pressure on these regimes, they might turn yet more totalitarian; at the same time, cooperating with them may turn out to be an effective factor in transforming them into democratic regimes.

One has to be especially naive to buy this reasoning. Not since the dawn of humanity has there been a more or less known case when a dictator – lightheartedly, of his own volition – has created a democratic regime in his own country. Has anyone ever uncovered in history a dictator, who voluntarily surrendered power, period?

Not only does a totalitarian regime oppress human spirit and reason, but in an equal degree it rapes nature as it barbarously devastates natural resources.
The unwise, predatory Soviet policy turned powerful rivers and reservoirs dry, eroded fertile soils, and destroyed unique flora and fauna. Chernobyl alone, besides bringing grief and suffering to hundreds of thousands of people, turned to waste many acres of fertile land, woods, and bodies of water for years to come. This tragedy demonstrated to the world the essence of an ineffective, vicious regime, which has sacrificed its people and natural resources in the name of prolonging its deathly agony.

Azerbaijan, too, suffered tremendous damages as a result of the Soviet regime's unwise policy: the Caspian

Sea was poisoned by industrial and household waste; fertile soils were ruined by chemicals; miles of steppe sunk in lakes of naphtha; the terrain scarred by stone and sand quarries, abandoned in haste; vineyards with rare kinds of grapes cut down, following the Kremlin's cartoonish anti-alcohol campaign; finally, several rare species of mountain goats and bears became extinct, having fallen prey to the hunting passion of visiting VIPs, who could not hit their target unless it was tied to a tree.

Many are problems of today's Azerbaijan. But the greatest one, the one that appears on the front pages of the world's newspapers, is the problem of developing the Caspian oil fields. The Republic's Government has signed contracts and agreements with leading oil companies of Great Britain, the United States, France, Norway, Turkey, Japan, Iran, and Russia.

According to the "historical contracts," signed in the past few years, the oil resources that, according to the research, can yield 3 billion tons, or 24 billion barrels, have been transferred to foreign oil companies.

In the more than hundred-year history of oil production in Azerbaijan, 1 billion tons has been produced, of which only 20 percent went to satisfy the republic's domestic needs. The rest of it was made available exclusively to the Russian Empire, and then to the Soviet Union.

Considering that Azerbaijan needs to produce 10 million tons of raw oil a year to meet its own needs, evidently 1 billion tons will last the republic 100 years. Why, then, just before the 21st century, should one rush to sign these "contracts of the century" and sign away the resources that belong to the Azerbaijani people who will live in the next 300 years?

Who will dare determine what natural resources will be vital to the Azerbaijanis who will be born in the next 10, 20, 50 years? Never before in world history, not even in the history of totalitarian regimes, has a Government sold off the property belonging to the generations of the next three centuries.

How could this happen?

How can a state, whose main purpose and duty to society and future generations consist in building a democracy, securing freedom of speech and conscience, and defending human rights – how could a state waste natural resources in this fashion?

"Contracts of the century" will yield happiness and prosperity, they say. When? To whom?

Transfer of oil reserves to foreign companies does not signify actual oil production.

It is possible that 100,000 or 200,000 tons of Azerbaijani oil will be exported. People will rejoice, slaughter lambs for shashlik, raise toasts to the health of their sage leaders. A naive man-in-the-street sees a flow of oil and hears a ringing of coins in his threadbare pocket. This may happen, but it will be only the first half. The second practical half will be nothing but a dream. And the longer we stay in this somnambular state, the longer the imaginary bliss.

But enough illusion. Let us face the bitter facts. Azerbaijan will never become a major oil exporter. The volume of oil produced in the world today – 3.2 to 3.5 billion tons a year – exactly matches the needs of the world community. This amount has been practically

191

unchanged in the last ten years, without noticeable fluc-
tuations up or down, and there is no reason to believe
it will go up substantially in the next few years. A trend
toward reduction is more likely, as developed countries are busily working on alternative energy sources.
Besides, both the production and transportation costs
in oil-producing countries of the Persian Gulf are half
those in Azerbaijan. If we take into account that the
Republic of Iran is moving toward democracy, that the
Iraqi regime is in its last throes, this may mean an ad-
ditional 500 million tons arriving at the world market
at reduced prices. If we throw in 100 to 150 million
tons of Russian oil, 50 million of Kazakh oil, 20 million of Uzbek oil, 100 million from Southeast Asia, and
the same amount from Latin America, it is easy to conclude that the economic policy of Azerbaijan – or any
other country – based exclusively on oil will end in a
debacle.

This is quite obvious. Then, what is the reason for
this policy?

The first thing that comes to mind: signing these
contracts may help resolve the problem of Nagorny-
Karabakh. In other words, economic levers will be used
to obtain the support of foreign states. This is a pipe
dream, as many have already discovered.

Three years that have passed since "contracts of
the century" were signed in September 1994 have seen
no progress in returning the occupied Azerbaijani territories and the solution of the Nagorny-Karabakh problem. There has been no substantial shift in the position
of the US and other Western states. The only change
has been the definition of the status of the area, which
has now been raised to the level of confederation. The

Dismantling of the Red Army Monument.

Mass Resistance. Photo Reuters/Corbis-Bettmann

Spontaneous Rally, Baku.

The Empire's Last Labor Camp.

Scarred Building.

Victims of Soviet Terror. Black January, 1990, Baku.

Mothers' Tears.

recent treaty between Russia and Armenia guarantees that the latter will be protected by the military power of the former. Thus, the problem of the return of the territories and the reconstruction of the integrity of the Azerbaijani state is in a dead end and, with the policies being pursued, no solution is in sight.

Following the collapse of the Soviet Union, all the former republics became members of the United Nations, whose charter unequivocally affirms the territorial integrity of member states. This principle is affirmed by the new states' leaders and their signatures, so yet another formal confirmation of the same principle at yet another summit is of no political value.

The "contracts of the century" were followed by over ten new contracts, which did not lead to any positive changes for Azerbaijan in the world arena. Whoever attributes various summits and signed international agreements to oil contracts is wrong. Every country, whether it has natural resources or not, conducts such meetings, which are the function of their foreign offices.

The second benefit of oil contracts is deemed to be an influx of investment into the Azerbaijan economy, which presumably would lead to higher living standards for the Azerbaijani population. We can already say with confidence that this has been another fiction. Compared with 1994, the living standards have fallen 50 percent; as for the investments, the statistics are open to interpretation. In 1994 there was practically no investment (about $1 million) in Azerbaijan, so with the oil companies having invested $200 million to date, the volume can be said to have increased 200 times. Yet the real criterion of foreign investment should be an increase in jobs for Azerbaijanis, and this picture is hardly rosy. In our estimation, in the last five years the total number of jobs has fallen 50 percent.

So what is the real objective here? The answer is clear.

In the first place, the oil resources will reduce or eliminate the pressure of foreign governments on the ruling regime.

In the second place, the oil contracts are meant to promote an illusion of a democratic environment for a nonexistent democracy and encourage certain foreign political leaders to lobby for the regime. I stress: lobby for the regime – not for the interests of the Azerbaijani people. This is how it's done. A certain well-known American public figure will meet the republic's opposition and lecture them: you're too young, you need stability instead of democracy, so don't rush. This is the irony: a person who has spent his life fighting totalitarian regimes suddenly makes a U-turn.

In the third place, as foreign companies are signing the contracts, it is made clear to them that they owe these contracts to one man only, and without him the contracts will become invalid. The oilmen pose a natural question: what will happen if this man is gone? The answer: even now, you must begin supporting my successor, who will continue to help you retain and expand your interests in our country. If someone else comes to power, the situation may well change, say 180 degrees, and you will be run out of the country. Here it is, a heartfelt dream of one person, based on the simplest logic and the conviction of plausibility of making it happen. The flip side of the dream is a tragedy of an entire people.

The truth is that the real objective of these contracts is not the happy future of the people, but a longer life for the totalitarian regime. Of course, the foreign leaders setting international policies may be temporarily deceived, but they can hardly be expected to base their policy toward a country on such primitive logic.

For example, protecting interests of American citizens who represent their companies abroad is certainly a cardinal task of the American Government. Yet American leaders can clearly see that supporting the totalitarian regime will mean great losses, both political and economic, for their country. In my mind, the United States, Western Europe, and the Russian Federation should be primarily interested, not in propping up a given person or regime, but in supporting the entire people, its democratic aspirations, and creation of democratic institutions. Only when Azerbaijan creates an open society, can the United States and any other democratic country have a steady and reliable partner in the region.

I would like to remind to those who prefer simple concepts that the US investment in Iran was a thousand times greater than it is in Azerbaijan, and the Shah's regime, which followed the logic described above, fell in two months.

Curiously, a small region like ours, in a very short time, was overrun by dozens of companies from all over the world, of various size and importance, some of which had nothing to do with oil business. All of them won bids, though the bids were never made open. Otherwise, how does one explain the presence of a small unknown company next to a giant like Exxon in an oil contract? In general, how many companies can reasonably participate in one contract? In what other country do ten to fifteen companies of various sizes participate in one contract? Isn't it bound to lead to negative consequences in managing the consortium? The companies understand it very well, so that some shares are already changing hands.

As a result, it looks like Azerbaijan has not so much sold as given away its deposits. A bonus is not a gift nor a selling price; sometimes it yields up to 200 to 300 percent profit, which is the kind of profit a company that sells its share in the consortium is bound to make.

Why is it that Azerbaijan is giving away its oil?

Everybody has a share of the above-mentioned contracts – with the exception of the Azerbaijan Oil Company. Originally, its share was 30 to 40 percent; however, soon it was given away or, rather, sold for peanuts. What is the real reason?

Of course, it is necessary and important to work with such foreign companies as Exxon, Amoco, BP, and others. Yet the contract must be iron-clad, so that the companies that signed it were confident about the fate of their investments.

For example, if in a contract Azerbaijan would have a 49 percent share, and Exxon, 51 percent, the result would be quite different. Why turn a business contract into a mass grave?

According to the first contract, Azerbaijan would own half the produced offshore oil. Yet this is a vague number, and one does not need a degree in economics to see that the sharing applies to the net profit, i.e., what is left after all the investment and maintenance expenses are covered. These expenses are so great that one cannot rule out a possibility of a zero net gain, or even a negative one, since much will depend on the world prices at the moment of sale.

I repeat: it is at least dangerous to lull the people with sweet talk of the "bright oil future."

As long as such policy is being pursued, neither this generation nor the next one will have a normal life. By giving away the natural wealth that God bestowed on Azerbaijan the regime will only cripple the generations to come. We will not be around for that, and little is asked of the dead. It is our children and grandchildren who will suffer the results of this irresponsible policy.

The vise of the totalitarian regime has gripped the people so tightly that today they believe they will ever live in freedom and civilization even less than they had under the Soviet Empire in the 1980s or following the bloody events of January 1990.

I recall the words of Mirza Alekper Sabir, the great Azerbaijan poet, who wrote at the turn of the century:

> The century strikes a conversation,
> But we do not join it.
> The cannons shoot,
> But we do not respond.
> The foreigners have launched dirigibles into the sky,
> And we still can't crank up a car.

Yet I do know and believe that my people are worthy of a life devoid of fear and slavery, of enjoying freedom and fruits of their labor, just like other worthy nations of the world. It is not that hard to crank up a car: one only needs experience of political struggle and a desire to live like human beings. And we have enough gas to fill that car, too.

2. MY VISION OF FREE
DEMOCRATIC AZERBAIJAN FACING
THE 21ST CENTURY

The 20th century saw global changes. The totalitarian Communist system fell apart, and mankind got a chance to build a democratic, free, open world. A new kind of world community has come about – an information or postindustrial community.

Members of the Club of Rome Alexander King and Bertrand Schneider narrated problems of and perspectives for this type of community in their report "The First Global Revolution" presented to the Club's Council.

The Club of Rome comprises intellectuals from all over the world, whose vision of world processes is not colored with either politics or ideology. This renders their predictions and interpretations particularly valuable.

Among the most important events of the last decade, the Club members included the following: the fall of the Soviet and East European regimes, reunification of Germany, and the Persian Gulf crisis caused by the Iraqi invasion of Kuwait. They link the importance of these events to the final result: on the one hand, the end of the Cold War; on the other hand, the rise of conflicts that were up to now concealed. They believe that, as a consequence, we will see more conflicts between rich countries and poor ones, between the North and the South.

Difference in economic levels, the contrast between extreme poverty of some countries and wealth and prosperity of others, may cause tensions and conflicts on and off in various locations. These trends are typical of the first global revolution that will determine the future of the planet. It took mankind tens of thousands of years to move from hunting and gathering to husbandry and farming; the industrial revolution that started in England two centuries ago is coming to an end. The global revolution will affect the fate of mankind in the next few decades; therefore it is important not to make any mistakes in implementing and managing it.

According to the Club of Rome:

> The new society emerges from the old one, which sometimes is archaic and disintegrating. Its evolution is complex and imperceptible; its manifestations are hard to interpret. This creates problems for decision makers in state politics and private enterprise and causes the thinking part of society to pose questions. The new society appears in flashes here and there, without an apparent relation between them.
>
> The global revolution has no ideological foundation. It is created by an unprecedented mix of geostrategic disturbances and social, economic, technological, cultural, and ethical factors. Their combination leads to unpredictable situations. In this moment of transition mankind faces a double task: to learn to govern the new world and to learn to avoid situations where the new world may begin to govern mankind. This involves carefully feel-

ing one's way to understanding the new world, with many concealed forces and the fog of uncertainty. Our task consists in representing vividly the world in which we would like to live; estimating material, human, and ethical resources; making our visions realistic and reasonable; and then rallying human energy and political will in order to successfully build a new global society.

Among fundamental modern changes, the Club's intellectuals list the transition to a market economy; the higher interdependence of states; the awakening of and gaining independence by ethnic minorities; dynamic growth of urban population; greater attention to population growth and environmental problems; scientific and technological achievements; intensive investment growth; international economic cooperation and greater influence and importance of banking structures. They also underscore the importance of three "problem zones" in accordance with Forrester's First Law: "In any complex system, regardless of the degree of evident reason, the collapse of one element or quality leads to the violation of the whole system."

Such "zones" are:

■ Transition from military to civil economy
■ Global warming and energy problems
■ Choice of optimal strategic directions for harmonious development of backward countries

Especially important here is the last point. In selecting an optimal direction of development for backward states, one should not fall back on tried and tested paths, but combine existing crafts with unique development paths. Government structures must encourage local initiatives, raise prices for local goods, and lower taxes for local producers in comparison to foreign ones. As for such international bodies as the International Bank, European Economic Community, and others, they should concentrate their aid on small-scale projects, supporting primarily local private entrepreneurs and businessmen.

The members of the Club maintain they are ready to provide intellectual assistance to the countries that choose democracy, provided the following principles are being observed:

- Broad public participation in choosing solutions to problems facing the society.
- Recognition of the fact that the coming positive changes must be reflected in the choice of motivations and values that determine people's behavior.
- Understanding that the behavior of a country, a state, a society, reflects and must reflect the behavior of individuals.
- Accepting the assumption that radical problem solution should come not from the heads of government bodies. Numerous, small-scale, wise decisions that reflect the new thinking of common people are necessary and vital for society.
- The guiding role of the principle that a privilege bestowed upon a person or a group must always be accompanied by concomitant high responsibility.

The tasks set forth by the Club of Rome are global and meaningful; its members' activities are noble-minded and evoke admiration and gratitude. Yet I see a certain flaw in their approach or, rather, a theoretician's predilection to complicate reality to a degree where one has a hard time getting out of self-designed labyrinths.

In principle I agree that the real-life exponential curve is different from the mathematical one in that sooner or later it reaches a saturation point. Afterward, it turns into a level plateau or a descending curve. Insofar as this applies to the development of modern society, I proceed from the following assumptions:

■ A democratic development path and a free market are the only progressive way for mankind.

■ Despite its complexities and difficulties of transition periods, the development of a democratic society constitutes forward movement toward a society of free individuals, toward a level where every individual's abilities can be employed. Herein lies the categorical certainty of this path, the confidence in its results, the inevitability of this path for the entire world community.

■ So great and inexhaustible is scientific and technological potential that at least in the near future the rate of progress in different areas will be comparable to exponential growth and development.

■ The existing religious, national, and cultural differences have resulted and will result in antagonistic conflicts due to the closed nature of societies unwilling to break away from their totalitarian past. In a free society, emerging contradictions will be resolved by civilized democratic methods, in keeping with constantly improving norms of harmonious development of all individuals.

I think that the experience "recorded" in various holy books and in philosophical works by scientists through history gives us reasons to believe that human society develops steadily and inexorably in a positive direction, retaining fundamental values that correspond to human nature and needs, while casting off specious and false values.

Moreover, when each intelligent individual realizes himself as a person, it is absurd and inappropriate to talk about uncertainty and unpredictability of a free society and disappearance of common human values. Harmonious development of each person is the only effective way to the harmonious full-fledged development of the society as a whole, despite all the problems and contradictions.

According to the Club of Rome, we may expect confrontations between the rich and the poor in the future and, on a greater scale, between rich and poor countries.

On this important problem, I'd like to say the following:

First, this problem has existed since the world began, and the poorer that the people are, the more cruel they are.

Second, rich societies are more fearful of such conflicts, since they have something to lose, while the poor do not. Therefore, aid to poor countries is an element of policy of civilized countries, especially superpowers. Naturally, the easiest and the speediest way to provide aid is through financial donations, but this is no solution, primarily since the donations become a burden on the public of the donor country and lead to their discontent. This would not be so bad if at least such donations could lead to positive results, but that is not the case.

A nation that survives for a long time on humanitarian aid develops a dependent mentality. It turns into a chronic beggar, and finds it hard to return to creative labor.

There have been numerous theories of human survival in this world. Although at the dawn of civilization, the total population of the planet was a fraction of today's, there were already theories that the earth could not sustain so many people, which was why we needed wars that would reduce the size of the population.

Strange as it may seem, these theories have survived to date. They were followed by new theories, which maintain that, since a modern war can destroy mankind, wars are no longer necessary; yet the planet cannot provide equally good living conditions for everybody, which makes the coexistence of the rich and the poor mandatory.

None of these theories seem to get it right. Our planet is capable of sustaining a population tens and hundreds of times greater than today's, so in the next hundred thousand years this threat does not exist. Whatever wealth the earth gives to man, it gets back the same amount.

A simple example: in the last fifty years, the population of the People's Republic of China has tripled, though its territory has not grown one square kilometer. Nonetheless, the living conditions of the Chinese have grown ten times. Longevity rose by 15 years. Today China makes up one-third of the world population.

Therefore, the world's advanced countries must develop a consistent strategy of eliminating misery and poverty in order to secure the peaceful coexistence of all countries and their own safety. This can be reached only by creating open societies and democratic rule in all countries. The developed countries' investments are safe in democratic countries, and this is the only way of eliminating poverty and misery.

Seven years after the collapse of the Soviet Union, even the most out-and-out liberals have forgotten something. Namely, the demands to create an international tribunal for the crimes committed by the Soviet Communist Party against their own people and mankind at large. These demands sounded in the days when many, if not all, revealed documents demonstrated the antihuman nature of Communism and the Party as the carrier of ideas aimed at physical and moral destruction of free people. By now these demands have faded without a logical resolution.

Mankind needed the Nuremberg trials in order to render judgment on Fascism on the basis of existing international laws, shared by the civilized countries. These trials were needed not only for the sake of those who had lost their family or been victimized personally, but for the coming generations as well. This became an historical lesson, condemning Nazism and its ideas of *Übermensch* and *"Über*-civilization" As the historical birthplace of Fascism, Germany repented in front of the civilized world and condemned Hitlerism not only in media articles, but with trials of leading practitioners of criminal ideology. This made it possible for Germany to become a genuine democracy, where objective conditions for Fascism's rebirth have been eliminated.

Not one republic of the former Soviet Union has held a similar trial of Communism as an antihuman, unnatural system. Not a single Communist leader has repented or publicly apologized for his participation in crimes; moreover, they continue talking about their deeds as if they had been acts of heroism. Many of these gangleaders today occupy top leadership positions, sporting liberal, democratic, or religious disguises.

It will take a considerable amount of progress in the new democratic societies to condemn the antihuman ideology of Communism and its leaders. The tyrants of the bloody regime are tied with the old dogma, of terror and demented adherence to the cult of the Father of Nations, the master of the turf, which they are recreating in their countries.

Starving, impoverished people of the former Soviet Union must not deceive themselves once again. They must not betray the memory of the millions executed. They must not plunge the world into fear and total lies once again. They do not have the right to do so.

People must prevent the burden of Communist "prosperity" from surviving into the 21st century. The international tribunal of Communism and its leaders, who are still trying to return to the past, must take place in this century.

There is every reason for such a trial to take place in Azerbaijan, whose people repeatedly, until the last moments of the Evil Empire, were victims of the ideology of lies and hypocrisy.

As I say these bitter words, I realize that millions of former Communists, deceived or cowered by the totalitarian ideological machine, are absolutely innocent of these evil deeds. I mean primarily the condemnation of the ideology of Communism as an antihuman phenomenon of our century.

Unfortunately, today in Russia proper, turned by the Bolsheviks from a prosperous land into a beggar, there are still "researchers" who try to prove that Stalinism was a mere deviation from the norm. In his book *The Rise and Fall of Stalin,* published in 1992, Fedor Volkov writes:

> The just society where power belonged to workers and peasants, the democracy that Karl Marx, Friedrich Engels, Nikolai Chernyshevsky, Alexandr Hertzen, and Vladimir Lenin had dreamed of, was established in the backward Russia after the Great October Socialist Revolution. Lenin's guards dedicated their lives to the people and served this cause honestly and unsparingly.
>
> Iosif Stalin had never been a true revolutionary. He dedicated his life to one goal: unlimited power.
>
> The power in the hands of the men of honor, ones who truly love their people, is a great boon for mankind. But unlimited power can be a horrible tool in the hands of an unworthy cruel dictator who loves only himself.

So, once again, they are trying to fool us with fair tales of Lenin's humanity, the leaders' dedication to people, of greatness and nobility of Communist ideas. These people have a short memory indeed. And that is yet another reason why the trial of Communism must take place without delay.

How do I see the future of independent countries building their states on the ruins of Soviet colonialism as they face the 21st century?

Provided the democratic principles are observed, the main trends will be as follows:

Political System
Having rejected Communism as a criminal doctrine, independent countries – former Soviet colonies – will proclaim an open democratic society as their goal. The task of such a society is to provide its citizens with equal opportunities for free development according to their free choice. The state performs a function of protecting the citizens' rights, social security for the disabled members of society, and guaranteeing economic development based on free-market principles. This must not become an empty promise, but the real content of society and the state.

Following the civilized model, three branches of government are established: legislative, executive, and judiciary. In the former Soviet republics, a parliamentarian or a presidential republic seems to be an optimal form of government. Yet in practice the presidential rule often becomes a variety of the Soviet model where everything was ruled by one person: the Party's General Secretary. Today these functions, in somewhat different guise, are performed by the President, who has even greater authority and practically no limitations. Before, there at least used to be a Politburo, and the republican chiefs could be berated by Moscow; but today's bosses are more powerful than hereditary monarchs or supreme priests.

The foremost role in the 21st century's independent states will be played by the main law – the Constitution – affirming the basic equality of citizens. There is no tautology here, since, according to Orwell, general formal equality assumes that "some are more equal," especially when "some" includes the dictator or his clan. In the open society, fundamental issues will be decided by the citizens freely participating in a universal referendum held in accordance with established legal norms with international observers present.

All international legal agreements and norms will be strictly observed, including the inviolability of existing borders, human rights, and freedoms of speech, conscience, and movement.

Economy and Resources

The main economic features of the 21st century society will include:

■ Liberalized economy; privatization of large enterprises on the shareholder basis; privatization of small and medium-sized enterprises; transfer of land to farmers according to the constitutional norms of protection of private property; encouragement of private business with lenient tax policies at the early stage of development of small and medium-sized businesses; priorities given to local investment; participation of state financial bodies in crisis situations occurring in the evolution of the free market

■ Modern banking system, a policy of taxes and credits, an insurance system modeled after that of civilized countries and objective economic laws of an open democratic society

■ Stable pension fund modeled after those in the developed countries; social-defense funds for the aged, disabled, and orphans; encouragement of charitable activity of local and foreign businessmen through stimulating tax and credit policy

■ Economic and legal measures of coping with crisis situations: inflation, overproduction, unemployment, and evolutionary disturbances in certain industries as a result of market development

■ Treating education, science, culture, health care, social welfare, and defense as priorities in state investment

■ Both traditional and new industries will be given priority in state economic policy: international tourism, pharmacological chemistry based on raw materials, health care facilities, high-tech machinery, modern electrical and electronic equipment, etc.

■ Ethical and legal norms of using natural resources that take into account national needs and responsibility to future generations; adopting laws that would ensure taking into account present and future national interest when national resources – land, oil, gas, gold, metal ores, water, air – are being developed.

Education

■ Since intellectual potential is the main national treasure, education should be made state priority number one, and this should be written into the Constitution. State funds should be used as much as possible to develop middle and high schools on the basis of national and international experience. Legal norms must be developed for protecting state and private schools; private investment in educational programs must be encouraged; students must be provided with necessary learning and living conditions; students must be involved in national volunteer activities. Special funds must be created to encourage talented youth and educate them in the world's best universities.

■ The world's greatest scientists must be invited to international seminars on vital issues in science and education.

■ Considering the importance of the teaching profession in the formation of the national intellectual potential, legal and ethical norms must be developed and implemented to define and guarantee teachers' rights. High professional requirements must be based on international standards; normal living and working conditions must be provided and maintained.

■ Youth's rights in the family, at school, and at work must be protected in accordance with international standards.

■ While educational facilities will be given a great deal of autonomy and their cooperation with their foreign counterparts from leading countries will be encouraged, high requirements will be placed on the quality of graduates, for which purpose the best specialists in education will be invited.

Science and Technology

■ Encourage and promote traditional fundamental and applied sciences: geology, oil production, oil processing, oil chemistry, physical chemistry, theoretical and applied physics, mathematics, linguistics, history and philosophy, theoretical and applied mechanics, cybernetics, medicine, biology and agriculture. Also, promote scientific progress in economic modeling and forecasting, biotechnology, political science, computer programming and technology, highly effective industrial production in various areas of the national economy.

■ Create conditions for scientific research on the academic level, encourage participation of scientists and students in international projects and programs, establish state and private foundations for financing scientific research in high-priority directions of the national economy and culture.

■ Design effective technology in oil processing, oil chemistry, oil production, machine building, food and pharmaceutical industries, and development of natural resources and mineral waters while observing environmental requirements.

■ In acknowledging the unique value of the Caspian Sea, create an international research center for protecting and utilizing this natural resource, source of life and existence for Caspian countries.

■ Provide state support for science and education in health care, history and culture of Azerbaijan and its language and literature.

212

Culture

■ Insofar as culture is an integral part of national intellectual wealth, make it a priority in social development; provide state support in developing theater, literature, art, athletics, and traditional folk art.

■ Combine preservation and restoration of traditional arts – music, painting, architecture, theater, cinema, and literature – with encouragement of modern cultural trends; participate in international forums and projects.

■ Using traditional and modern arts and culture, implement a combined restoration program in the regions currently occupied by neighboring militarists and establish cultural education centers in the liberated territories.

Environment

■ Develop ethical and legal protection standards for the unique Trans-Caucasian region and its various climate zones on the basis of international standards, scientific achievements, and reasonable use of natural resources. Programs of state and private bodies will be directed toward revival, preservation, and development of national parks and preserves, and sanitary ecological areas.

■ Develop multipart protection programs for bodies of water, land, and unique fauna and flora, treating it as part of national wealth.

■ Encourage private investment in land, sea, and air environmental-protection programs.

Public Values and Priorities

In recognition of common national values as the most important moral and ethical criteria, an open democratic society encourages universal humanist themes reflected in cultural, educational, philosophical, and religious achievements: the Torah, the Koran, the Bible, and the best works created by mankind. Despite the claims that a modern liberated society of free people has lost common values and stimuli, the true values of a healthy human society are goodness, empathy, justice, tolerance, freedom of spirit, welfare – as opposed to greed, violence, hypocrisy, lies, immorality, cruelty, moral and material impoverishment.

The above categories will replace the dogmas created by the Party apparatchiks, the dogmas that limit individual freedom and turn an individual into a robot. These categories will become the norms on the freely chosen path of development and self-improvement.

These values are nurtured by family and society, by church and school, and become an integral part of human moral conviction and conscience.

These values are the stimuli of progress and free development of both an individual and society at large.

Conclusions

1. Even in its "softest" manifestation, a totalitarian regime is an antihuman system that leads entire nations to a tragic outcome, suppressing the nation's free spirit and intellectual creativity and replacing them with fear.

2. A totalitarian regime eliminates the middle class by suppressing all opportunities to realize one's intellectual and business abilities. As a result, a different society is formed. The top layer, 1 or 2 percent, is a servile, weak group, including those close to the dictator. They obey no law and use various privileges at the expense of the lower tiers. The bottom tier amounts to approximately 90 percent of the population, comprising those constantly searching for means of subsistence. Between the two is an interlayer consisting of creative people, businessmen, traders, and craftsmen, who from time to time manage to sell their product and thus rise above the impoverished masses.

3. A totalitarian regime does not really accept an opposition nor any other form of alternative thinking. Since in modern conditions, the regime must maintain a democratic image in order to be admitted in international institutions, it cannot afford to suppress the opposition completely. Instead, it does everything possible in order to turn the opposition into an amorphous, disorganized, impotent mass. To this end, the more sober members of the opposition and those sympathetic to them are terrorized to the extent where not only actions but even thoughts of action are suppressed. As a result, the opposition is reduced to an insignificant group of career-minded politicians who have failed to find shelter in the dictator camp and who naively count on taking power after a change of government. There are also individual fanatics who dream of power. History teaches, however, that ultimately the fanatics' ideas are doomed and supporting them will not yield meaningful gains.

4. A totalitarian regime cannot exist without censorship, managed by the dictator productively and selectively. Even members of the cabinet may be criticized, to any extent, but only if the dictator is indifferent or hostile to them. A person breaking the rules of the game may be punished for bribery and corruption. Thus is created an appearance of a campaign against these negative phenomena, but it is aimed at a naïf. This is how a democratic image of the regime is formed: there seems to be plenty of newspapers, with plentiful criticism – hence, democracy "flourishes." Nonetheless, protecting himself and his coterie from the fire of criticism with the tamed censors, when something goes wrong the dictator spreads the word: the officials are to blame. What can he do? It is human to err – the dictator excepted – and he has too much workload to monitor everybody.

5. The main condition of prolonging the life of the regime (and every dictator dreams that his regime last forever) is driving the people to extreme impoverishment. Repression must be used to this end for several years in a row, so that people will get used to this as a natural condition. This makes governing the country easier and simpler. If a certain category of employees, say doctors or teachers, are driven to near-starvation, the dictator tosses them a carrot, like a 10 to 15 percent pay raise; next, it does not take a major effort to have them sing paeans to the dictator, extolling his humanity and droning about their unredeemable debt to him.

This is a long-range plan. Its implementation is tangible with the leftovers from the sale of natural resources that belonged to this and the coming generations. These leftovers will be generously distributed to the citizenry to prevent them from starving to death or swelling with hunger. For that, the regime will be thanked with deep repeated bows and wishes of long life for the Most of the Mostest.

6. A totalitarian regime has no need for strong national companies, stockholding companies, and simply rich national capitalists ready to invest in the national economy. It is the other way around. Preference is given to a foreign "businessman," mediocre and with a con-man reputation in his own country (I do not mean large oil and other companies known the world over). All the doors to all areas of the national economy open wide for this gentleman.

7. Each citizen is "enabled" to commit a crime, big or small, needed to survive. The smallest lapse in the future may turn this into a "case" against him and his family. The entire society lives in fear and expectation of punishment.

8. In order to distract the public from the idea of the necessity of opposing the regime in order to lead a normal life, the regime artificially creates tension in the country and fabricates "events" that shake people up. The regime exposes "failed" coups d'état, attempts on the President's life, embezzlements of State property, finds public enemies, and fights them while finding new ones. For variety's sake, it also serves up good news: cooks the data about the national economy and better living conditions, stages new contract-signing performances, spreads rumors of their historic value – and, of course there is the role of the dictator in all of the above: without him none of it would be possible. Statistics, falsified from top to bottom, are always added on to make these stories more convincing.

9. In contrast to Stalin's period with its primitive technology, TV propaganda acquires the foremost value as an instrument to pronounce "great deeds." Day and night, people's brains are washed with recitals of pre-fab collective "decisions" in support of the dictator and his deeds, thus creating an appearance of mass public support for the regime. An individual, whether he is a worker, a farmer, a beggar, or an intellectual, who bears discontent deep inside, will never suspect others of sharing his feelings, since the TV screen creates an appearance of the whole country backing the dictator. The appearance is reinforced by dragging respectable people into the TV hysteria. Should this person refuse under any pretext to take part in the show, he and his family will immediately pay the price. "Aha, so Mr. X has said *No*. Well, let's see how he (his son/nephew/brother-in-law) will manage to be elected into Parliament (appointed as section head/academician/body shop manager)." Naturally, he himself stands to lose whatever position of privilege he has.

10 In order to hold on to their privileges, all officials from top to bottom are expected not only to show warm support for the regime and the dictator personally, but also to "organize" support from their subordinates, families, and neighbors. As a result, beside tens of thousands of "active" supporters, the dictator enjoys "passive" – but seemingly broad – support from hundreds of thousands of others. In order to step up the excitement, the regime finds big-mouthed orators, with a competent command of language and literature, whose own works, or works by their family members, will be promoted and paid well for. Should they succeed in befogging the already unclear minds of the masses, the awards will find their "heroes."

11 The regime promotes success stories – workers, farmers, businesspeople, or people without fixed occupations – as examples of what one can achieve under the regime. For such a person, the regime is no obstacle – rather, it is a beacon, an arrow on the road.

12 It is my deep conviction that without radical social reform, without an open democratic society, without turning democratic principles into a vital necessity, without a legal framework, without equality of all people under the law, one cannot secure freedom, human rights, creativity, business activity, and inculcate in people the conscience of main national tasks. It is the same vein as you cannot have a good harvest without abundant rain, how all things alive need clean air, how a green seedling needs the bright sunshine.

The sooner every member of society sees his bright future as inseparable from freedom – and only freedom, freedom of personal initiative, freedom of conscience; the sooner one accepts democratic society as the future ideal; the sooner one perceives the contents of this book – the sooner the days of happiness and joy will arrive for him and his family, both present and future.

A man is born only once, and everyone has a right to live his life, so short from a historic point of view, in a human fashion – enjoy life, bring up children. The Soviet slogan, *Live however you can so that the next generation lives in abundance,* remained just that – a slogan, just like some religious people would say, *The harder your life is in this world, the happier you will be in the next one.*

In a country whose population has never been happy through its history, the future generations will not be living in abundance either. Each person who finds his way out of the totalitarian regime has a right to live freely and happily, and no one has a right to take it away from him. Nations that for centuries underwent suffering and destruction, that made innumerable sacrifices for the sake of freedom, have deserved a right to escape a life of hardship. Therefore, every person must decide his future for himself, and no one must stay on the sidelines.

13 We must cast off the question, *What can I do by myself,* which leads to passive behavior. If everyone adopts this slogan, it will the slogan for an entire people, who will be posing this rhetorical question. Remember: state institutions are created following your wishes. State leaders and officials live at your expense. It is your taxes that form the state budget and pay the official's salaries. This is the contract between the people and the institutions; you support the state. It is the state's duty to promote your prosperity, to provide you with health care and education, to pay the salaries of doctors and teachers and the pensions of retirees – in other words, to provide services the way you would like. According to this contract, the state is also responsible for the inviolability of the territory and the defensive capacity of your country.

Today, your money pays every official's salary. It is his duty to guard the law, to protect human rights and freedoms, to defend you against organized crime.

This is your state. You have created it, and all citizens, all governing bodies signed the main document of the land called The Constitution. You signed it by voting for it. Every person who occupies a government position must be guided by the adopted Constitution, no one can violate it, and specially designated officials must stop any violations. If these officials themselves violate the Constitution, this will mean they fail to fulfill their obligation to the public. It will mean that the rulers are violating the agreement between themselves and the public. Then you will have the right to remove violators from their office by means of an election.

14 There is neither a top layer nor a bottom one at the elections. The basis for your vote for your officials, from local ones to the President, must be that *he* will be serving you, and not you serving him. You will be the ones to impeach those who do not fulfil their duties. Each elected official is responsible to his electorate. Do not forget: you have no obligations to him. Your only obligation is observing the laws and the Constitution.

15 All leading positions, from city and village mayors to district leaders, must be elective. A country cannot be governed by fiat.

16 At all enterprises, in both the private and the public sector, candidates for leading positions should be nominated by the collective – the workers and the staff, or by the council they have elected. The collective cannot exercise control over the director if he has been appointed by order. Any incompetent person may be appointed to a leading position.

17 All problems arising from relations between citizens, or between the citizens and the law, etc., must be solved by neutral or totally independent authorities. The entire justice system must be created in accordance with your proposals and your choice, and its decisions must apply to everyone without exception.

18 It is impermissible to ban rallies, strikes, speeches against the regime, workers' actions against the management, etc.

19 It is impermissible to use censorship to ban freedom of speech and alternative philosophies, whether it applies to the majority or the minority.

20 The legal statutes that create problems in establishing political parties, that are prone to different interpretations and are written in a subjective manner, should be nullified. It should be possible to establish parties whose programs are not aimed against human civilization.

21 Media must be free, and treated equitably by the state. The state should not finance any privileged media. All media should be supported in equal measure without favoritism.

The state must inform the public of its actions through information releases, clarifying its position in the media of its choice.

22 By no means should the state suppress the opposition, or the parties holding opinions different from the official one.

To use a metaphor, opposition parties are an arm of the government. If the ruling party is the right arm, then the opposition is the left one. You cannot cut off the left arm, for tomorrow they might have to trade places. A one-armed nation is half as productive. Mistakes made by individuals are radically different from the errors committed by nations. Even great mistakes made by common individuals cannot affect either a nation or a small group of people. Yet the smallest errors committed by the nation may lead to great trouble for the future generations.

Today we are witnessing a tragedy of the people caused by errors committed throughout their history. Enough is enough. We have neither the right nor the time to commit new errors. Let us try to live, to think, and to act in such a manner that neither we nor the future generations will find ourselves in a yet more tragic situation tomorrow. I see only one path, one direction: democracy, the freedom of man, the open society.

BIBLIOGRAPHY

Ambrose S. "When the Americans Came Back to Europe",
  International Herald Tribune, May 28, 1997.
Huggani H. The Legasy of Partition. *New York Journal,*
  August 15, 1997.
Kents P. Bertran Russell. London, 1985
King A. Schneider B. The First Global Revolution.
  NY, Pantheon Book, 1991.
Koch A., Peden W. The Life and Selected Writings of
  Thomas Jefferson. NY, 1992
Mao Tse Tung. Mao's Road to Power, NY, 1985.
Machiavelli N. The Prince. A Mentor Book. Los Angeles, 1985.
Miller D. Popper Selections. NY, Princeton University Press, 1985.
Naisbitt J. Global Paradox, NY, 1995.
Despeignes P. "Economist Jose Pinera", *Investor's Business
  Daily* , March 27, 1997.
Popper K. The Open Society and its Enemies.
  Princeton University Press, 1968.
Schumacher E. Small is Beautiful, NY, Harper Perennial, 1989.
Soros G. Soros on Soros. NY, John Wiley & Son, 1995.
Yunus M. "Soul from the Ground Up", *Noetic Sciences
  Review,* Spring, 1997.
The Wit and Wisdom of Winston Churchill, ed. James C. Humes,
  NY, Harper Perennial, 1995.

Азербайджан. Крепости. Замки. Баку, 1994.
Белади Л., Краус Т. Сталин. М., 1990.
Бжезинский З. Большой провал. New York,
  Liberty Publishing House, 1989.
Бунин И. Окаянные дни. М., 1990.
Волков Ф. Взлет и падение Сталина. М., 1992.
Вольский Н. Наследники Ленина. М., 1991.
Гумилев Л. Древние тюрки. М., 1993.
Гумилев Л. Тысячелетие вокруг Каспия. СПб., 1993.
История и сталинизм. М., 1996.
Китаби Деде-Горкуд. Бакы, 1988.
Лобанов М. Сталин. Тайные страницы истории. М., 1995.
Низами. Искандер-намэ. Бакы, 1985.
Соломон Г. Среди красных вождей. М., 1995.
Солоухин В. Расставание с идолом. Нью-Йорк, 1991.
Сумбат-заде. Азербайджанцы — этногенез и формирование
  народа. Баку, 1990.
Штейнберг М. Уроки Закавказских войн.
  «Новое русское слово», 17 июня 1996 г.